Life After Birth

A Memoir of Survival and Success as a Teenage Mother

Summer Owens

iUniverse, Inc.

New York   Bloomington

Scripture quotations are from the New Living Translation version of the Holy Bible.

Some names included in the book are pseudonyms.

iUniverse books may be ordered through booksellers or by contacting:

iUniverse
1663 Liberty Drive
Bloomington, IN 47403
www.iuniverse.com
1-800-AUTHORS (1-800-288-4677)

ISBN: 978-1-4502-2103-0 (sc)
ISBN: 978-1-4502-2102-3 (ebook)

Printed in the United States of America

iUniverse rev. date: 06/25/2010

Acknowledgments

I want to first thank God for keeping me when I wanted to give up and for pushing me to be the best mother and woman I can be.

Although many times I felt alone throughout my journey as a teenage and a young, single mother, I always had people supporting me and praying for me. Sometimes in big ways and often with the smallest gestures, countless people have played roles in helping me overcome my obstacles. Several of them are named throughout this book. However, it would take a lifetime to name all the people that I have been blessed to encounter throughout my life so if your name is not listed in the book please forgive me and know that your contribution to our lives has not been taken for granted.

Thank you to Teddy Wright of Wright Touch Photography for the fun and therapeutic photo shoot that resulted in the main image for the cover of this book. In this photo, my son is the same age that I was in the smaller photo taken by mom capturing the first moment I held him when I was fifteen years old.

And thanks to everyone who has encouraged me over the years to pursue all of my dreams including sharing my story through this book so that others can see how God has blessed me and how He can bless others, including teenage mothers.

Dedication

To my loving and, most of the time, patient and understanding son, Jaylan. You endured and accomplished everything right along with me. I know it hasn't always been easy or fun, and I know at times it's been sad and lonely; but, I hope one day you realize that I did my very best to make the best life I could for us as we grew up together.

Table of Contents

Foreword

It's funny how things happen. Growing up we often imagine our lives unfolding in a certain way, and then a few unexpected curve balls are thrown at us. We must then decide if we will dodge them, let them hit us and take us out, or if we will catch them and throw them back. One of these curve balls was hurdled my way on my fifteenth birthday, and nine months later I was a mother. I was not the only teenage mother at the time, and I certainly would not be the last.

Teenage pregnancy is prevalent and many times the consequences are long-lasting and devastating. In most cases, young girls become mothers alone, with only a "father" to conceive but not to help with caring for the child. In addition, teen mothers usually give up on any goals they may have had before pregnancy. Busy taking care of babies, many teen mothers don't finish high school or pursue higher education, setting themselves up for a lifetime of struggle and dependency on public assistance and other people.

This book is definitely not a celebration of the epidemic of teenage pregnancy. There's nothing fun or glamorous about having a baby as a child. In fact, it is limiting, embarrassing and hard. Unlike my friends who came home from school, and eventually work, and did whatever they wanted-whether it was watching a television show, talking on the phone, working out or just laying around doing nothing; my evenings were dictated by my son's needs. Helping with homework, driving to basketball practice, disciplining bad behavior, hearing about his day and preparing for the next one were the activities that consumed my evenings. Even talking on the phone to friends was a luxury that was limited to the time it took me to drive to pick up my son from his aftercare program because as soon as I saw him, my attention had to go to him. Going on dates was out of the question. Having a normal life as a young person with the huge responsibility of motherhood is a tremendous challenge that I strongly encourage teens to avoid.

Not only does the teen mother's life change, but so do the lives of her entire family. Like the new mom, the family has choices to condemn or to support her. Once the baby is born, everyone must move forward for the betterment of the lives of the mother, the baby, and the father if he is involved. No one benefits from putting down the teenage mother. As a matter of fact, entire families can end up having to support the teen mother and her child for years because the proper support was not given on the front end. Instead of being reminded of their mistakes, teen mothers should be encouraged and told they can still be, do and have whatever they choose. They can still be successful and independent, creating a great life for themselves and their children.

No matter how much teens are warned against it, teenage pregnancy happens. This book is simply an acknowledgement of the fact and evidence that teen pregnancy does not mean a death sentence for a young woman's dreams. By sharing my story, I hope to provide inspiration and motivation for teenage girls who are already or soon will be mothers. For those girls considering abortion, I encourage you to choose life instead. Not only should you choose life for the unborn baby, but you should also choose life for yourself once the baby is born. Regardless of the circumstances, God wants us all to live and to prosper. The challenges I endured and the accomplishments I realized have provided me with a story that I hope will encourage young mothers to continue to set goals and pursue their dreams and create the best lives possible for themselves and their children.

My life has not been one that would be described as easy though. In fact, it has been nothing like I imagined it would be. From the age of fifteen, I was embarrassed when people asked me how old my son was then looked at me knowing I was too young to have a five-year-old, ten-year-old son, etc. I was ashamed because some of those people already knew exactly how old I was and astonished that sometimes others would even ask me my age. Finally, I got past the humiliation of being a young mother and realized I didn't owe anyone any explanation. It was my life and no one else's, and I had made a decision to make the most of it. Rather than feeling ashamed for having a ten year old son when I was twenty-five, I was proud and thankful for what I had accomplished *in spite of* being a teenage mother.

God wanted me to be completely transparent and show other teen mothers what is possible. The life I have created with God's help is rewarding, full of love, grace, family and a focus on the Lord. Over the years I have shed many tears and still do today, but I am thankful for every aspect of my life, especially the trials that helped me develop into a strong, independent woman who knows and loves God and all that He can do. Because I realized success is a choice that takes deliberate effort and that there can still be a meaningful and fulfilling life after the birth of a child, I chose to pick up a bat, a board, a hammer, a book, and whatever else I could find and make every attempt to knock my curve ball out of the park and into another country.

Introduction

My warm blood ran down my skinny arm and sprayed everything on and around me. There was so much blood that the clumsy nurse had to change my once pale blue gown and the white sheets on the long, narrow hospital bed. In an attempt to insert an IV in my arm, she had somehow ruptured one of my tiny, always hard-to-find veins causing blood to decorate my body and my bed. My heart nearly beat out of my chest. I was fifteen years old about to somehow push a huge basketball out of a hole in my body that I felt could only handle an orange at best. The nurse cleaned the blood, and when my heart stopped racing, I realized I had forgotten about the contractions that only minutes before had crippled me. Panicking from the pain of the needle and seeing my blood all over the place made me forget everything. However, once the IV was safely in my arm and the blood was cleaned up I remembered the contractions and was fully aware of the pain again.

I didn't hear my own screams for the audible beeps of the monitors competing with the instructions of the doctor and the nurses. Always calm, my mother manned a post at my head. Standing and sometimes sitting by my side, she gave a few words of comfort but mostly quietly crocheted or watched television until the main event began. "It'll be over before you know it," she said with a half smile that was probably holding back tears. I figured she was thinking, *I just can't believe we're here. My baby is having a baby, and she's still a baby. How are we going to do this? I have children at home already and now another one. How did this happen to us?*

The stirrups felt like ice chips pressed against the ashy soles of my small feet, but that was nothing compared to the crippling pain at the foot of my belly. In the nick of time the doctors helped me into a sitting position. As I arched my back and gripped the bed rail, she pierced the small of my back with the epidural. Conflicting feelings of fear from seeing the long needle and the need for pain relief were resolved without my feedback and I was lowered back onto my pillow. As my lower body began to go numb and I no longer felt the pain from the contractions, I was relieved that the needle won the fight. But there was no time to rest. Soon after the relief kicked in, it was time to get to work. I had fully dilated, and it was time for the moment we'd all been waiting for. I clinched the bedrails and started to push. Through my knees which were spread as wide as an eagle's wings I saw my doctor's head as she reached inside of my vagina in an attempt to pull the baby down. "We can't see his head yet. He's actually turned sideways," she calmly stated as she asked me to keep pushing while she tried to pull the baby in the right direction for a vaginal birth. "Come on, Summer. Give us a big one now."

"Ugggggghhhh!" I grunted again as I pushed as hard as I could for as long as I could. When my eyes weren't on the doctor seated between my legs or on my mother by my head, they were on the small, round clock on the wall behind the doctor trying to turn my baby around so that it could come out of my fifteen-year-old vagina. I watched the clock wondering how long the ordeal could possibly take.

After a long hour of grunting and pushing, my doctor broke the news to me, "Summer, this baby's stubborn. We're going to have to perform a C-section."

Before I could fully turn my head around to show my mother my frightened face, I was being whisked away to the operating room. My baby would be cut out of me. I was so scared that it felt like I had stopped breathing and my heart stopped beating as I lie on the hospital bed being rushed down the hall to the operating room.

Once there, the nurses strapped my arms down to the bed, placed an oxygen mask over my mouth and nose, and positioned a small, blue sheet vertically above my stomach so that I could not watch as they cut me open. Additional anesthesia was administered through my IV. It was all happening so fast that I didn't have time to even think. I began to panic again when the oxygen mask started to smother me. At first, shock had taken my breath, but now the oxygen mask was doing that. I couldn't breathe, and I began to feel the pressure as the doctor cut into my abdomen. I knew I was surely about to die either from suffocation or the stabbing that was taking place on my stomach. Actually, part of me wanted to die.

Moments later at 2:24 AM, the doctor pulled out the baby I had been carrying for the past nine months and handed it to my mother who sat quietly in a chair near my head. As the nurses stitched up the incision on my abdomen, I lay peacefully on my back with my eyes closed in shock over what had just occurred. When I finally got the nerve to open my eyes and turn my head to look over at the baby - my baby, motherhood felt more real than I could have ever imagined. The baby was beautiful. I was scared. It was official. I was a mother, and I was only fifteen. A new life had come from me, and this meant a new life for me.

The Innocent, Little Girl

"O Sovereign Lord," I said, "I can't speak for you! I'm too young!" -Jeremiah 1:6

"Ouch!" I cringed and yanked my head away as my aunt's friend gripped the few, short pieces of coarse, black hair that were still left on my head.

She yelled, "Summer, stop moving!" smacking my hand with the yellow, plastic comb in her right hand and maintained her tight grip on the braid she had started in my hair with her left hand as I sat on the floor with my head between her knees. She was trying to cornrow my hair because that was about all that could be done to it since I had pulled most of it out. Like my mother, my sisters had long, thick ponytails, but I wore little pigtails or braids all over my head of short, coarse hair.

For as long as I could remember, I had been twisting and pulling out my hair and sucking my thumb. Whenever I was bored, sad or just thinking, I stuck my left thumb in my mouth and rested my pointer finger on my top lip or on top of my nose. With my right hand, I found an area on my head that still had hair and begin twisting it until, eventually; I gave it a nice tug and pulled out a patch of hair creating another little bald spot on my scalp.

Although she could look at my head and deduct what was happening, I tried my best to keep my habit a secret. I overheard my mother explain to one of her friends, "I'm not sure what's wrong, but they say she has a nervous condition that makes her suck her thumb and pull out her hair. I really don't know what to do about it." I didn't have a clue what she meant.

All I knew was that I was different. My hair looked liked a bird had pulled it all out in a frantic search for bird seeds someone might have hidden on my scalp. Eventually, my mother grew sick of looking at her daughter's bald spots, grabbed a pair of scissors, and cut off the spikes of hair that remained on my head. She cut it as low as she could to try to even out my hair

1

with the empty patches in hopes that new hair would soon return there. With my new haircut, I received lots of questions but the worst came from a little girl in my kindergarten class. She innocently yet ignorantly asked, "Um, are you a boy? I thought you used to be a girl."

Later in my first grade year, my stepfather got a job as a restaurant manager in Jackson so we moved there from the small town of Bolivar. My family consisted of my stepdad Steve, my mother Curtistine, my sister Brandy who was born eighteen months after me, and me. A few years after moving to Jackson, my mother had Jessica, then Stephen and finally, Tevin. Steve had a daughter, Janelle, who lived in New York and was a few years older than me and visited us during the summer. Also during the summer, I visited my father Cecil and his wife Peggy who lived in Nashville. Peggy had two children who were older than me too. All together there were a lot of children, but I still sometimes felt alone and isolated in my own little world.

On my last day of school in Bolivar, I waved goodbye to my kindergarten classmates and braced myself for my new school. Once there, child after child leaned over to other students placing their hands over their mouths and their neighbors' ears and not so softly whispered, "Is that a boy or a girl?" as I entered the classroom.

I often wore dresses to school to provide the children with a clue of my gender thinking the dress would scream, "I am a girl!" After finally proving that I was a girl, I still didn't feel right. Something was still wrong. Because my family didn't have a lot of money, I often wore my mother's, oversized plaid dresses to school. On my feet every day were my favorite, black, patent leather slide-ins with a black emblem on the top. I wore them with stockings, with socks, with dresses, with jeans, as dress shoes, and even as sneakers.

Once I got to Jackson, I initially had no friends, but eventually, I found a couple as I moved through elementary school. In first grade I met Rebecca, and in third grade, I met my best friend, Chinitra. We attended the same school and lived in the same neighborhood. Chinitra's house was right down the street from mine. After school and on the weekends, she came to my house or I went to hers to ride bikes or play dolls. If we weren't doing that, we were listening to Tevin Campbell or Mary J. Blige cassette tapes or walking around the block. Sometimes Brandy and Jessica joined our play especially when were coloring or playing hopscotch. My brothers were usually inside playing video games or with action figures. During the summer, we dawned our shower caps to keep our hair dry to "get wet" which meant creating our own water sprinkler by taking turns spraying the water hose on each other.

 Although I had a couple of friends, I was still very shy and hated how I looked. Boy hair, bucked teeth from years of sucking my thumb, and wearing my mama's clothes weren't the only problems. My clothes barely touched my skinny frame earning me the name, "Stick". Some children at school were still calling me a boy. My protruding teeth brought on the beaver and rabbit jokes. "Want a carrot?" never got old to some students who could barely get the question out without laughing.

 By the time I was in the sixth grade, a group of girls started the "I Hate Summer" club. One of the rules for the club was for no one to talk to me or sit with me at lunch. I knew I was not pretty or popular, but I didn't understand why basically the entire class proclaimed they hated me. Even girls who had been my friends for the past few years had joined that stupid club including Chinitra, my "best friend" since third grade. That year I was in what was called a split class which was about half fifth-graders and half sixth-graders. I was a sixth-grader, and even the fifth-graders wouldn't talk to me. I had stopped pulling out my hair, and it was even growing back. I had also stopped sucking my thumb, but the bucked teeth were still there because my family couldn't afford braces. I didn't even go to the dentist because we didn't have dental insurance. My dad and my stepmother had bought me some new clothes including a stone-washed denim jacket and jeans set and even a pair of nice tennis shoes. Being nice and even having a few nice things didn't dissolve the class-wide club though.

 But I had bigger things to worry about. In the midst of the drama with the children who proudly proclaimed that they "hated Summer", I started my menstrual cycle. Although I didn't have any friends to discuss the news with, I had overheard that some of my classmates had started their periods earlier that year. The girls who had not weren't as mature so I was excited when mine finally came. Getting up from the top bunk bed that Brandy and I shared one Saturday morning, I saw an oblong circle of blood on the sheets. I checked my panties. Yep, it was from *there*.

"Ma, what do I need to do? I'm bleeding you know where." I asked my mother as she lay in her bed.

She didn't move a muscle or get excited as she said, "Get a pad in the closet in the bathroom."

"Okay," I replied not completely sure of what I was supposed to be looking for. I found them and pulled one out of the package and nervously placed it in my underwear. I thought, *Yes, I'm finally a woman!* I didn't realize the responsibility that came with having my period or with calling myself a woman.

Soon after I started my period, the leader of the "I Hate Summer" club started her period and eventually the club disbanded. I guess we were all growing up. Finally, out of my lonely prison sentence with only one girl named Patricia who was brave enough to be my friend, I began to be accepted by my class. I didn't know if it was because they figured out I wasn't so bad or maybe it was because I was the only person in the whole school who knew someone in Saudi Arabia.

Serving in the Persian Gulf War, my father kept in contact with me through letters, pictures and video tapes. No longer the black sheep of the class, I was unique and special and had interesting memorabilia to share. Each week I stood before the class showing off my latest gift from my dad from Saudi Arabian money to Persian Gulf T-shirts. For Christmas that year, he sent a special video addressed to my entire class. With holiday music playing in the background, he gave a tour of his living quarters and even showed us parts of Saudi Arabia. "Summer, your dad is so cool," one classmate stated.

I smiled with relief and replied, "Thanks. I know." I was no longer the pariah of the class. My dad was cool; therefore, I was cool.

By middle school, my hair had grown out some, and I was able to wear ponytails. My only friend moved away, but I made a couple of new friends including two girls named Bilicia and Destiny. Chinitra was my friend again too. They were all smart girls who did their schoolwork and made good grades, but they were all cute girls too and were popular with girls, boys and teachers. With these friends, I was a little more comfortable with myself and felt better about being around others too.

However, as my body continued to develop, I got another physical condition that caused me to become shy and withdrawn again. My skinny frame quickly began to spread, and my skin didn't have time to adjust. I developed stretch marks on my hips and on the back of my legs behind my knees. "Summer, who wrote on the back of your legs with a black marker?" I couldn't believe one of my classmates would say that, but that confirmed I had to keep my legs covered. To hide them, I mostly wore pants and avoided skirts completely. However, I still wanted to be like my friends and do what they were doing, and they all wanted to be cheerleaders.

I tried out for cheerleading with them, and we all made the squad. That was great except for the fact that we wore short cheerleading skirts. Not only did we wear them at games, but we also wore them to school on game days. I moved throughout the hallways quickly trying to get to my classroom to sit down. Leaning against the lockers pretending I had nothing to hide shielded my legs from the stares of students who would make fun of me. I looked forward to cold days when we wore jogging pants underneath our cheerleading skirts.

I hated those stretch marks, and I did everything I could to get rid of them. "Bran-dy, com'ere! I need your help." At night before I went to sleep, I stretched across my bed on my stomach and Brandy would reluctantly rub vanishing cream along the dark lines on my legs.

"Summer, it's not working anyway. I'm tired of doing this," she complained, but I couldn't give up. I tried cocoa butter too; however, nothing seemed to work.

And if that wasn't enough, it was also during this time that I developed acne. The bumps on my face had personalities of their own, and they never wanted me to be comfortable around other people. Walking around the house with Noxzema on my face for what felt like hours to let the medicine *really* work, I was determined to conquer the beasts on my face. Although I was told that I was pretty, I could never look anyone in the eye and always stayed as far away from people as I could so they couldn't clearly see my face.

I was insecure in so many ways and convinced myself that I was just an ugly girl, but I eventually started to feel a little better about myself. Although I still had buckteeth, I somehow managed to get compliments on my smile. That always amazed me. My face had started to grow to fit my huge, protruding front teeth. Smiling as I tied a red ribbon around my ponytail, I was happy to be like the other cheerleaders. Yes, my hair had finally grown. The stretch marks were a part of me that I didn't try as hard to hide anymore. I thought it was just me, but I learned that most people had similar stories of insecurities and struggled with learning to like how God made them.

Lessons Learned:

♥ **Children can be cruel but don't realize how they make others feel.** Don't let other people's opinions determine actions. Many times, people mistreat others out of jealousy and not understanding that person rather than a true dislike for that person.

♥ **Treat people with kindness.** Everyone has issues and insecurities they may be dealing with that others may not know or understand.

♥ **A person's worth should not be determined by how they look on the outside.** Take time to know and appreciate people for who they are and not for how they dress or look.

♥ **Be thankful for everything.** Looking back over my life, I'm thankful I was not one of those children who had it all because many of them don't have much now! Some of the children I knew were given everything they wanted while I was thankful to have the things I needed and occasionally got something extra I wanted.

♥ **Learn from the past, and don't dwell on shortcomings.** It didn't matter how I grew up, rich or poor or with or without friends. What mattered for my future was what I learned from my upbringing whether it was how to do things or how *not* to do things. Allow life's circumstances to shape a positive future rather than inhibit growth. Appreciate the good and learn from the bad.

A Giving Spirit

Give, and you will receive. Your gift will return to you in full—
pressed down, shaken together to make room for more,
running over, and poured into your lap. The amount you give
will determine the amount you get back. -Luke 6:38

The summer before starting high school, my mother convinced me to serve as a youth volunteer at the mental institution in Bolivar where she worked in human resources. When we moved to Jackson years earlier, my mother never changed jobs so she still worked in Bolivar which meant an hour-long commute to and from work every day. That summer, it meant the same for me. The director of volunteer services who led the volunteen (teen volunteer) program, Susanne, had worked with my mother for years and one of the nicest and most caring people I had ever met. When I started participating in the program, I thought she was just a sweet person, but as events in my life played out, I discovered she was truly an angel just like the ones she collected.

Standing before a room full of teenagers, Susanne led the orientation. My palms were a bit clammy and my heart raced slightly as she spoke and I began to feel overwhelmed by the entire experience. *Why did I agree to do this?* For starters, I knew I would get lost on the huge campus while walking to the different buildings that I needed to visit to get my jobs done. I wondered, *What if I run into a patient? What will they do to me?* My fears were soon quelled when we took a tour of the campus which brought it down to size for me. It was not nearly as big or as complicated as I thought. During the tour, we encountered several patients who were friendly and obviously happy to see new, young faces.

"Hi young lady," a chubby female patient with short, messy gray hair asked "You gonna be working out here with us?"

"Yes, ma'am," I nervously replied.

Over time, it got easier for me to talk to most of the residents of the hospital, and after walking the campus alone my

8

first week and getting lost a few times, I never got lost again. As a thirteen year old, the adjustment to learning a large campus and a new place was a good experience that I repeated many more times in my life.

As I got comfortable venturing the campus from my mother's office in the administration building to other buildings such as the cafeteria and the other office buildings, I also adjusted to my actual job. Although it was boring and monotonous at times, I enjoyed my tasks of filing, shredding, typing and other light office work because the people that I worked with showed me how much they appreciated my help on a regular basis.

"Thank you so much for making these labels, Summer. It would have taken me all day!" One of my supervisors regularly exclaimed.

Eventually, I understood how doing little things make a big difference in accomplishing the overall goals. Because I felt so appreciated, I made sure I did my best no matter what I was doing and looked for ways to show them I enjoyed working with them and appreciated the experience I was getting.

However, it took perseverance to spend my entire summer giving my time away when I wanted to make some money. Many days I did not feel like going to work with my mother. After a few days in the middle of the summer asking, "Ma, do I *have* to go today?" and getting the response, "It's up to you," followed by a look that said, "I'll be disappointed and so will everyone else if you don't," I stopped asking and just went to work without complaining. Driving there took us an hour which meant it took an hour to get home after spending an entire day laboring. I was a teenager and that summer I had to get up by 6:00 AM every morning to get to work by 8:00 and work all day without pay and not get home until after 6:00 PM.

As we drove back to Jackson in my mother's light blue minivan that did not have air-conditioning at the end of the day, sweat rolled down our faces and inside our clothes during the hot summers with temperatures usually exceeding 95 degrees. Riding with all the windows down didn't seem to make much of a difference. Usually my mother was light-hearted and funny with jokes to keep everyone laughing, but our miserable ride home each day usually kept us both quiet and concentrating on staying cool. Exhausted from the long drive in the unforgiving heat, when we got home we staggered into the house, cooled off, and then prepared to repeat the routine again the next day.

The long summer was challenging, but it was worth it once I understood how the sacrifice I made then actually paid much more than any job I could have worked that summer. First of all, I learned how it felt to have a job. Although it was without pay, I made an hour-long commute, worked a nine hour work day with an hour lunch break, and made an hour-long commute home just like my mother. I also learned the importance of responsibility and commitment. The only similar experience I had gotten up to that point was a month the previous summer where my friends and I were able to get summer jobs cleaning dorm rooms on a college campus that a church was using for a teenager retreat. Cleaning refrigerators and toilets were my responsibilities while someone else handled vacuuming and other people managed the rest. I hated it, but I wanted to earn money. That summer, I realized that foregoing the instant gratification of money for an experience that did not pay was much more valuable in the long run.

Working as a volunteen instilled a new attitude of gratitude in me. Like most teens, I had only focused on me and what I wanted and did not have, and how I wanted to look. In walking from building to building and participating in various activities with other volunteens and sometimes mental patients, I encountered lots of different types of people who probably wished they could have had the things I had or even been me. The interaction with the patients gave me a greater appreciation for my own mental health and the mental health of my family and eventually of my own child.

Finally, the experience taught me that hard work and dedication, no matter the job, pays off in the short-term *and* long-term. From doing what I thought were menial tasks, I learned to do my best no matter how unimportant I might think the request might be. Doing a good job for the employees, not only gained me compliments, but it also earned me recognition, awards, and most importantly a college recommendation that also helped me earn a leadership scholarship.

At the end of each summer, the hospital held an awards program to recognize the volunteers. I was given the opportunity to create the programs and signage for the ceremony. At the time, computers and programs for creating signs and banners were not an option so I drew everything by hand and used my new friend the typewriter to create the programs.

Susanne led the ceremony announcing the various award recipients. Standing with a plaque in her hand, Susanne stood behind the podium and spoke into the microphone, "Our next award recipient has not missed a single day of work all summer. Riding from Jackson with her mother every day, she certainly deserves recognition for her commitment to help us. Come on up, Summer Owens." As the audience applauded, I approached the stage in my burgundy pants suit that camouflaged my wide hips to accept my award. Returning to the stage a second time, I also received the most iniative volunteer award.

My first summer as a volunteer was a great experience that I repeated after my freshman year of high school. That summer, I competed with other youth volunteers throughout the state for the JC Penney Golden Rule award for outstanding volunteer service. I lived in Madison County, had volunteered in Hardeman County, and at this ceremony, the Mayor of Shelby County acknowledged me as a candidate for outstanding teen volunteer for the entire state. The huge Peabody Hotel Ballroom was filled with chatter and the scraping of plates and clinking of glasses before the mayor began, "It is unusual that we find teenagers willing to sacrifice their time to help others...".

He continued to talk, but in my nervousness I tuned him out and wondered if it were really possible that I might win the pure crystal flame-shaped trophy he held in his hand. "This young lady..." *my first clue*, "never missed a day on the job..." *second clue* "and developed activities and programs for mental patients in Hardeman County..." *Okay, he has to be talking about me.* "Summer Curteece Owens, we're proud of you." I was so nervous that I didn't think my knees would bend to let me climb the stage. I couldn't believe I had won this prestigious award simply for helping people. When my mother had asked me to volunteer for the summer, I did not do so for the recognition or the awards. In fact, I didn't expect to get anything out of it for myself and really didn't think I had much to offer anyone either. However, I gained even more than I ever gave.

Lessons Learned:

- ♥ **Appreciate life and having a healthy mind and body.** Working around people with mental challenges made me appreciate my own mental health and taught me how to respect and communicate with people not as fortunate as me.

- ♥ **Big things can easily be brought down to size.** I was scared when I looked at the huge campus and even considered backing out of the commitment to volunteer, but after only a week I knew the whole campus and felt silly that I was ever concerned.

- ♥ **Simple work makes a big difference.** My small projects contributed to the success of big projects and something as small as a smile or time to talk to a patient or coworker made an impact but took very little effort.

- ♥ **Show appreciation.** When I showed my appreciation, people were even more pleasant and willing to help me too.

- ♥ **Make a good impression.** Although all I was doing was simple office work, I made sure I did it well. I was on time for work and always put my best foot forward. Although awards and recognition were nice, they weren't my goal. A good reputation and referrals were the best pay I could have ever received.

The Challenges of High School

Walk with the wise and become wise; associate with fools and get in trouble. - Proverbs 13:20

After my first summer as a volunteer, I left middle school behind me. I couldn't believe it. I was finally in high school. Like most teenagers, I had felt "grown" for a few years already but then it was finally official. I was now really grown, in my eyes at least.

On the first day of school as ninth graders, Chinitra and I caught the bus down the street from our houses. When the big cheese pulled up to our new home away from home, we stepped off the bus and into our futures. Initially intimidated by the huge campus that housed three large buildings connected by a long crosswalk, I remembered my summer as a volunteer and calmed down knowing I would soon know the entire campus like the back of my hand.

Feeling like a lost puppy trying to find my way home, the first few days of my high school experience were chaotic. Academic classes were held on the east and west campus buildings which seemed to be a mile apart, and technical classes were held in the vocational building which was located between the academic buildings. Once my friends and I made the trek from building to building, the next challenge was finding the right classroom and making it through the door before the bell rang.

Unlike in elementary and middle school, in high school I had several friends, but my problems with myself resurfaced. I still didn't know how to control my acne, and braces hadn't magically appeared in my mouth so my bucked teeth were still a part of the Summer everyone knew. It seemed like the warnings were true that my stretch marks wouldn't go away so tiger stripes remained on the back of my legs and other places that I, thankfully, could more easily hide. My size four shirts and size fourteen pants revealed a disproportionate figure with hips too wide for my small frame.

Although my problems that seemed huge at the time still bothered me, I did my best to cover them and my feelings about myself. I wanted to create the appearance that I was normal. I often borrowed clothes from one of my older,bigger cousins because she had large jeans and long shorts that came nearly to my feet helping me camouflage my huge hips and cover up my stretch marks. Being a good student and making good grades helped me become popular with the teachers. Having good friends that other students liked helped me become popular with students. However, I was hiding part of who I was behind the big clothes and sometimes even fake laughs.

Before going to high school, I tried out for cheerleading with my middle school friends, but this time I didn't make the cut. I still wanted to find a way to get involved on campus because I knew school was so much better if it wasn't just about schoolwork. Although I was still shy, I joined several campus organizations from Beta Club and honor societies to student government and the yearbook staff. By far, my favorite was the yearbook staff. Even though I didn't like writing stories for the yearbook, I loved taking pictures and planning layouts for the book everyone would have for the rest of their lives.

Jackson was where my school and my friends were and was clearly home, but Bolivar was still an important place for me and my family. Although we had moved to Jackson, we still had family in Bolivar and my mother still worked there so we still visited often. Throughout my childhood, my mother and her twin sister, who had moved to Jackson too, and all of their children piled into my mother's van and headed to Bolivar to visit our grandparents. Once our grandparents moved to Jackson and the children in our families continued to grow in number and in size, the trips became fewer. However, occasional visits were still a necessity.

Typically the visits were to see family, but sometimes the trips served other purposes. On one visit, my mother dropped me off at the high school to meet up with my cousin at a basketball game. My cousin introduced me to a ninth grade boy named Markus that she knew and thought that I would like.

"Hey, Mark! This is my cousin, Summer, that I was telling you about," my cousin blurted across the bleachers without warning.

He walked over to the two of us, and I immediately looked down hiding my face from embarrassment and to keep him from seeing all the bumps and blemishes that kept me socially stunted for years.

I finally looked up and shyly said, "Hey," then asked the rhetorical question, "She's crazy, ain't she?"

He laughed and started making his way down the steps of the bleachers saying, "Well, it was nice to meet you."

I felt like an idiot because I didn't, well couldn't, say more to him. My stupid face. However, I was relieved when my cousin called me the next day.

"Summer, Mark asked me to give him your number! He was wondering if you liked him because he said you wouldn't even look at him, but I told him you did. He said you were cute! He'll probably call you tonight."

He did, and our long-distance romance began. I was crazy about Markus, and talking on the phone was not enough. I looked for any excuse to get my mother to go to Bolivar so that I could see him. When we got together, we had a kissing festival, but that was it. I was still a virgin and wanted to save myself for marriage.

Lessons Learned:

- ♥ **Associate with positive people.** I sought and found friends who had similar priorities to mine and who wanted more out of life.

- ♥ **Self-love is critical.** Once I began to accept my appearance for what it was, I cared less about what others thought of me eventually learned to appreciate myself and all my imperfections.

- ♥ **Self-realization is key.** As a teenager, I didn't know who I was or what I wanted. Life experiences and time revealed these things to me, but understanding myself and my desires was the key to setting and achieving goals.

- ♥ **Attitude determines aptitude.** I learned that my attitude determined what I would be and how far I would go in life, as well as how happy I would be and even how much money I would make. Although I was inherently stubborn, I made every attempt to be positive and learn from others. Manipulating my own nature as best I could, I turned my stubbornness into determination.

What is *It?*

I knew you before I formed you in your mother's womb. Before you were born I set you apart and appointed you as my prophet to the nations." -Jeremiah 1:5

A nice breeze flowed through the windows of my mother's minivan filled with her five children and her mother on May 15, 1994 as we drove down the highway to the church we somewhat regularly attended in Bolivar. Nervous and excited at the same time, I clutched a small, blue plastic Wal-mart bag tightly in my left hand as I rushed into the back entrance of the church wearing a T-shirt, shorts and tennis shoes. In the bag were a dress, a pair of stockings, and a pair of black, patent leather shoes that I would change into after I dried off. I was about to get baptized.

I anxiously awaited my turn hoping that I wouldn't drown when Pastor Gregory Hammond laid me back into the water. Never learning how to swim, I practiced how I would hold my breath when it was my turn. I put on my shower cap to keep my hair dry and when Pastor Hammond leaned me back, I pinched my nose tightly and closed my eyes just as hard but still panicked when my body was submerged in the water. Before he pulled me up, I jumped up and nearly out of the pool. He and the rest of the congregation stifled their laughs, and he continued with the baptisms. In the bathroom, I dried myself off and changed into the clothes from the bag and found a seat next to my mother where I watched the rest of the service. I was saved and baptized and made it clear that I was on God's team. Pastor Hammond warned me, "Now you really have to watch out because Satan is upset with you. He's gonna come after you hard." I really didn't know what he meant and I didn't want to look ignorant by asking, but I soon found out.

A week later on May 21st, I attended the Bolivar Central High School graduation with two of my female cousins. I didn't know any of the people graduating, but I knew Markus would be

17

there. After the graduation was over, we congratulated the graduates and I talked to Markus before walking over to the building where a birthday dinner was being held in my grandfather's honor. In the small town of Bolivar, no destination was really beyond walking distance. The party was for my paternal grandfather so a lot of my dad's family was there. Some I knew, and a lot I didn't. Because I lived with my mother, I was not as close to his family as my mother's. She did a great job of taking me to see my dad's parents and I even spent the night with my dad's youngest sister, Pat, who was only nine years older than me, sometimes when I was younger.

At my grandfather's dinner, I met an uncle from San Francisco that I had never seen or even heard of before. On this trip to Bolivar, he brought one of his sons and his son's friend they called Poppey. My dad introduced me and my cousins to my uncle, and my uncle in turn introduced us to his son and his friend. It was nice to meet my family, and I even thought my new uncle looked a lot like my dad, but my first impression of Poppey was that he looked like a bad combination of Bushwick Bill from the rap group Ghetto Boys and the comedian Chris Rock. The first thing out of his gold-toothed mouth to my cousin was, "Man, your cousins are fiiiiiine!" as he leaned back and looked me and my other female cousins over with his x-ray eyes. We said thanks, but my thank you was overshadowed by a frown because I found him very unattractive to put it nicely.

We stayed at the dinner for a few hours and then headed to my Aunt Pat's house. Pat was my young, fun aunt that all the nieces and nephews loved to hang around. That night, I stayed at her house and so did one of my female cousins. My cousin from San Francisco and his friend came over too. We all laughed, joked and talked through the night and into the early morning. By about 2:00 AM when Pat and her boyfriend retired to her bedroom, my California cousin expressed his real reason for coming to Pat's house. He didn't want to get to know his aunt and cousins better. He was interested in my other cousin who was my cousin on my grandmother's side of the family and not related to him.

They started kissing in the living room, and I felt uncomfortable watching so I left the room and went into my aunt's spare bedroom. At first I didn't realize it, but by the time I got in the room I saw that Poppey had followed me. The lights were off in the bedroom so I wasn't disgusted looking at him as he sat on the bed next to me and began talking, comparing huge San Francisco, California to little Bolivar, Tennessee. Then I could see the silhouette of his head shaking with disbelief as he said, "All the girls in your family are so pretty. Man, all of y'all are fine."

I mostly listened to him thinking, *But you are so ugly you probably think every girl is fine.* I was also surprised to hear him use the southern term "y'all".

Eventually, I scooted all the way to the wall and lay back on the bed and just listened to him talk. He kept talking as he lay down beside me. I tried to move even closer to the wall. He rubbed my head, and then touched my stomach, and I cringed as he did, but I didn't make him stop. I don't know why. I didn't like him. I didn't even enjoy his touch, but my mouth didn't move to say stop yet. He quickly made his way to my shorts and unzipped the navy blue Duckheads I had changed into after the dinner. He proceeded to put his fingers inside of me, and I let him. I guess it was because I was an insecure teenage girl who wanted some attention. The lights were off so I couldn't see him so I forgot about his unattractiveness. Before I knew it, he was stretched out on top of me, and I was trying my hardest to push him off. My aunt was asleep, and I didn't want to wake her or draw attention to what was happening so I quietly yelled, "Get off of me," as I struggled to push him away.

He never said a word. Only I did. "Get off," and "Stop" were repeated over and over until he decided to get off of me on his own because I was just not strong enough to force him off of me. After what was probably only a minute or two but felt like an hour-long ordeal, he finally got off of me.

The bed was pushed into the corner of the room, and I slid back, knees to my chest seeking the protection of that corner. I couldn't believe what happened next.

He whispered, "Can we do it again?"

I thought to myself, but my mouth couldn't form the words, *What! Do what again? Are you serious? Do it again? It, like sex? Did you actually put your penis inside of me? But I'm a virgin and didn't feel a thing.*

He didn't say another word as I ran to the bathroom and sat on the toilet trying to push out anything that might have gone inside of me. As I sat there pushing as if I was giving birth, I cried replaying the past thirty minutes in my mind over and over again trying to figure out if "it" had really happened. I was never loud because I didn't want to wake my aunt or even disturb my horny cousins in the living room. I was stupidly considerate. I don't know if my cousins had sex or not, but I was mad because the only reason I was even in the room with Poppey was because I wanted to be away from them while they made out.

It was their fault, but what really happened? I never felt his penis inside of me, but he said, "Do it again." Didn't that mean we had done *it*? I had never had sex before so if I had just had sex that meant I was pregnant. That's what happens when people have sex, right? That was part of the reason I had never had sex with Markus. I don't know how long I stayed in the bathroom, but I didn't ever want to come out. When I finally did, I ran back into the bedroom where he no longer lurked. The three of them were in the living room, and I didn't even look at any of them as I closed and locked the door in attempt to close myself off from the world. Confused and ashamed, I quietly cried myself to sleep.

The next day-actually that same day-was Sunday, exactly one week after my baptism. My mother was supposed to be picking me up from Pat's house to go to church, but when she called to ask if I was ready for church I said I wasn't ready and asked her to go without me. I couldn't face her or the church. I felt disgusting. I tried to look at myself in the mirror, but I couldn't even do that. Even though no one really knew what had happened, I was embarrassed. I didn't even really know what happened. This was the worst day of my life. It was also the day I turned fifteen; a birthday I'd never be able to forget.

Ashamed of what I had allowed to happen to me, I kept the trauma of that night to myself. I didn't tell a soul-not my mother and not even my closest friends. Putting the pain and confusion of that night in a little box and pushing it as far back in my closet as I could so I'd never have to see it, I tried to make myself forget about everything that occurred that night and not worry about what could come from it. That trick didn't work, and I continued to replay the scene in my mind over and over, but I needed the camera to focus in closer so that I could see what really happened.

I wondered, *Had I actually had sex? Did it really happen? Did my struggle to get him off of me prevent me from feeling him? If it did, then I could be pregnant or have a disease. I just don't know. Was all of this my fault anyway? This doesn't make sense!*

As events unfolded in my life and I began to talk about what happened, the few people I shared my secret with all wanted to know one thing-why didn't I press charges. Nonconsensual sex equaled rape. I had told him no and even tried to push him off of me, but he ignored me and continued anyway. When it took place, I was too embarrassed to tell anyone, and a big part of me felt like I caused it to happen. Knowing I didn't even like him, I shouldn't have even let him lay a finger on me, but I did. Did this mean I was asking for sex? I recalled sympathizing for victims of rape on television shows and movies who were put on the stand in courtrooms and humiliated as they relived their torment. Weeping as they attempted to divulge the details of their ordeals, these victims were still sometimes not believed.

Would that happen to me? Would I have to sit in a courtroom talking about my horrible birthday present just for people to ultimately say, "She asked for it"?

Unlike rape I had heard of before, my situation wasn't necessarily "violent", although it should have been. I could have done more to prevent it. I shouldn't have cared about waking my aunt. In fact, that should have been my goal. I knew he was on top of me and trying to put himself inside me, but I never felt it so I didn't think "it" happened. Not until he said, "Can we do it again?" A million thoughts on what I should have done constantly raced through my mind.

Finally, I accepted that I could not change the past, but I could make myself forget about it. I decided that instead of dealing with my feelings, I would suppress them and pretend like that night didn't happen.

Even in trying to forget, I still felt guilty and had to make it up to someone. Although Poppey had forced himself on me, I felt like I had cheated on Markus. Markus and I had broken up over something silly, but I still cared about him and in my mind he was still my boyfriend. After many long kissing episodes, we had never had sex because I was saving myself for marriage. Once Poppey violated me, I felt filthy and decided that waiting until I got married to have sex was pointless because it had already happened to me, but it didn't involve the only boy I liked.

Putting on my brave face, I nervously told Markus what had happened that night. My plan was to tell him what happened and then experience sex with someone I loved and forget about that other night. Purposely sparing him some of the painful and embarrassing details, I began. "Markus, he got on top of me and wouldn't get off. I pushed him as hard as I could, but he was so heavy. When he did get off, he asked me if we could do it again, but I promise I didn't feel anything so I didn't know what he was talking about. I don't know what really happened, but..."

Markus interrupted shaking his head, "I already know what happened, Summer. Dude been bragging to everybody here that he had sex with the finest girl in Bolivar. He said you wanted it and you liked it. Summer, you were supposed to be my girl and you did this but you wouldn't get with me."

Not quite crying but close to it, Markus was obviously hurt because he really believed I had consensual sex with a stranger and that I had been holding out on him. I couldn't believe that jerk, Poppey was lying on me and bragging and making it seem like I wanted him. I told Markus to make myself feel better, but then I felt even worse. I was hurt, angry and even more confused. After hearing my side of the story-the truth-Markus wrapped his arms around me and nearly squeezed the life out me as he looked at me with a half smile letting me know he was okay. No additional words left his lips. He just held me. Markus' hug turned into a long, passionate French kiss and then he began to pull up the short, flower-printed dress I purposely wore to his house. Then *it* finally happened. I had sex with Markus. Rushing to get done before his mother returned home, we were finished with the awkward and uncomfortable act in a matter of minutes with him pulling out before he ejaculated. Young and dumb, we did not use protection and birth control was not on my radar because I was not really sexually active. It felt so weird, and I obviously still wasn't ready for sex. I was trying to comfort myself though. I had given myself to someone I loved and could finally put the events of my last birthday in the past.

Lessons Learned:

♥ **Once Satan sees that someone is on God's team, he will surely bring on the trials and the tests.** Get ready for the changes and the challenges that will come.

♥ **Make smart decisions.** I never should have been in a dark bedroom with a person I had just met, and I should never have let him touch me at all. I paid the costs for those decisions for the rest of my life.

♥ **Teenagers don't usually know as much as they think they do.** I thought I knew everything, but I was so ignorant about sex and its implications on my life. My ignorance brought unnecessary pain and confusion.

A Major Shift

Do not judge others, and you will not be judged. Do not condemn others, or it will all come back against you. Forgive others, and you will be forgiven. - Luke 6:37

A couple of weeks after the incident, my mother bought me a round-trip bus ticket and I headed to Nashville for my regular summer visit to my dad. Although we always planned for two weeks, we usually only survived one because I was a teenage girl with a bad attitude at times. As an adult, I could recognize that. My dad was in my life, but not regularly enough to tell me what to do. At least that was my opinion, so we often bumped heads. Packing for this trip, I prepared for my menstrual cycle that was due to arrive while I was there. I added twenty maxi-pads to my suitcase. Anxious to use every, single one of the pads, every time I used the bathroom I looked down expecting to see blood in the toilet or when I wiped myself. When I didn't, I pushed a little harder to force the blood out that I knew was waiting to come.

After my Nashville visit was over, I returned home to Jackson with the same twenty maxi-pads I had taken to Nashville almost two weeks earlier. I began to rationalize why I had not received my not-pregnant confirmation, *When was my last period? I must have remembered it wrong, and I'm actually not due until next week. Oh, well, Summer, you know you're cycle has always been irregular and could come at anytime of the month. You've just been really stressed out, and stress will throw off your cycle.*

Even though I was convinced my period would come soon, in the back of my mind I still knew I could be pregnant. That's what happens when people have sex, right? Even though I never felt Poppey inside of me, over and over in my mind I could hear *his* voice saying, "Can we do it again?" I grabbed my stomach and covered my mouth because I felt like I had to vomit, not because I was pregnant because I wasn't, but because the thought of his words and what had happened made me sick. I did feel Markus, but none of his sperm went inside of me. No, I couldn't be pregnant, or could I be? Please no.

In the tiny bedroom I shared with Brandy, I stood in front of the full-length mirror that was nailed to the back of our door. Looking at my fifteen-year-old face that looked more like a twelve year old's face, I shifted my eyes to my stomach and began to rub it. Brandy sat on the floor gazing at me with a puzzled look on her face. She didn't say a word as I rubbed my then flat stomach from top to bottom. I questioned my thirteen year old sister to see what her response would be, "Brandy, what if I was pregnant?"

She shrugged her shoulders, rolled hers eyes, and flared her nose giving me a look that said either, "*Are* you pregnant for real?" or, "You play too much. That's not funny." I didn't know the answer to the question I asked her either.

In June, I started volunteering at my mother's job as I had done the past two summers. When my cousin who had introduced me to Markus asked my mother to drop her off at the health department on our lunch break, I decided to join her. She was a volunteen too and had arranged for a ride back to the office. She was sexually active, and we all knew it. Her mother had put her on birth control, and she was just getting a check-up and refills. Acting as if I was just tagging along with my cousin, I figured this trip to the health department was my only opportunity to be tested for any sexually transmitted diseases I might have contracted from *him* without involving my mother. If I could help it, she'd never know anything had happened to me.

I wasn't concerned about pregnancy because I knew my period was going to start the following week if not sooner. Right?

After sitting in the waiting area of the health department joking around with my cousin, the nurse called my name and led me back to the examination room. I had never been examined as a "woman" before so I did not know what to expect. In fact, it had been years since I had even seen my pediatrician. I explained to the nurse that I wanted to be tested for STD's.

She instructed, "Okay, sweetie. First, you need to give me a urine sample." As she pointed to the plastic cup in her right hand, she said, "Fill this cup up to this line and meet me back in here. The bathroom is right over there."

I followed her orders peeing in the cup and placing it in the little window for urine specimens and then returned to the tiny room where I sat swinging my legs from the examination table as I waited for the results and hoping he had not given me any diseases when he touched me. I wondered how long it would take her to test my urine for that.

As I sat on the table, I thought, *No, I still don't have my period, but I know I'm not pregnant. I just need to make sure I don't have herpes or anything else. I couldn't be pregnant. Just because he asked if we could do it again didn't mean we had sex, right? Sex had to be with someone you liked and the first time it had to hurt. There was even probably supposed to be some bleeding too, right? With Markus, he did not ejaculate inside of me so there couldn't be a baby. So, no, I can't be pregnant. But maybe it's possible I have a disease. Gross! But I need to know so I can fix it.*

Playing out hundreds of scenarios of disease and pregnancy in my mind, I was relieved when the nurse interrupted me when she re-entered the cold room. The relief didn't last two minutes as she nonchalantly, as if she did it one hundred times a day, relayed, "Well, sweetie, your pregnancy test came back positive." No emotion emanated from her pale, stoic face.

My mind began to race again. *I haven't even taken a pregnancy test yet. Have I? I thought my urine specimen would tell her if I had a disease or not. Was that the pregnancy test?* I was fifteen and just didn't know. No one had ever talked to me about sex other than the conversations I'd had with my friends, but they didn't really know any more than I did. We were all just guessing. Then reality hit as I sat on the edge of the examination table no longer swinging my legs. In fact, I didn't move at all. My mouth didn't move either but the conversation in my head continued, *I really am pregnant. I really am pregnant! What are you going to do? I didn't even have sex with him, but I know that guy, Poppey, did this to me. I should have let Markus get me* pregnant if I was going to end up pregnant anyway. Now, I have a baby in me by someone I don't even know. What am I going to do?

The nurse must have heard the question I posed to myself because after a moment of external silence but internal chaos, I was asked, "Well, sweetie. What are you going to do?"

My lips could not form words, but the pressure from my heavy heart was relieved some when I let out the cry that had been building up since the nurse dropped the bomb on me. Apparently, my cry was heard throughout the halls of the health department because moments later my cousin rushed into the examination room and held me as I cried. She had heard the rumors and around town about what had happened to me, but the nurse said what I couldn't, "She's pregnant, hon."

When I came up for air from crying, the persistent nurse asked me again what I was going to do. Without hesitation, my lips mouthed, "I have to have an abortion," and I continued to cry a little softer with disbelief.

What had I just said? Was this real? I know abortion is wrong and goes against everything I believe in, but how can I ruin my future by having a baby now. Much less by someone I don't even know. No, I can't do this. I'm not married, and I can't have a baby if I'm not married. This is not my life. I'm dreaming. No, this is a nightmare. Wake up!

I had done so many things right and was on the right track. I was doing well in school and had been recognized for my volunteer work. Adults at my church thought I was a good example for their children. My conversation with myself continued, *I'll be so embarrassed walking around pregnant. But abortion is so wrong. But what will everybody think and say about me? But I was going to be successful. But the baby won't even have a daddy. What if it looks like him? How can I have a baby and go to school. What will my mama say? What will my daddy do? I can't do this. I want a good life. I will not be a statistic-another teenage girl throwing away her life by having a baby. No, not me!*

Emotionally tortured, I knew what I had to do. There was no way I could have that baby. I was pregnant by a stranger and would be a parent alone. I didn't even know his name. All I knew was the stupid nickname I heard my cousin call him. And I knew that he was on his way back to San Francisco with the cousin and uncle I had just met and, at that moment, wished I never had.

With my young mind set on having an abortion, I composed myself and returned to my volunteer job where my mother would soon see me. Someone my cousin knew who worked at the health department had already agreed to take us back to work so I didn't have to face my mother until 5:00 PM when it was time to make the hour-long drive back to Jackson. Once I got back to work, I grabbed a huge stack of paper from the pile of confidential files that needed to be destroyed and retreated to the basement to spend the next few hours at the shredder hiding from everyone. I had about four hours to clear my blood-shot eyes and conceal my conflicted heart before encountering my always pleasant mother. I wanted to keep her that way. Climbing into the back row of the van, I said, "Ma, I'm so tired. I'm just gonna lay back here so I can stretch out and go to sleep."

"Oh, okay," she responded a little surprised because I'd never done that before on our ride back to Jackson.

At least I tried to go to sleep, and I pretended to be when I was not. I figured this would keep her from looking at and talking to me too much and being able to tell that something was wrong. When we finally made it home, she noticed my puffy, red eyes as I rushed into the house.

"I just woke up, Ma. They're always like that then," I answered before she could pry too much.

I scurried into the house, grabbed the phone and stretched the cord across the hall from the kitchen into my bedroom and closed the door as tightly as I could with the cord wedged in the doorway. A cordless phone would have been like water in the desert for me because I didn't want everyone in the house to know I was on the phone. I called my three best friends to let them know my life was over. After a few minutes of fidgeting with the phone, I dialed the first number.

"Chinitra…"

"Hey, girl. What's up?" she replied.

Behind tears, I stuttered, "I'm p-pregnant."

She burst out laughing and screeched, "Stop playing. You really do play too much."

I enjoyed making my friends laugh at times, but I was certainly not joking this time. I wished I was. At that moment I couldn't deal with her disbelief so I just told her I wasn't playing and needed to go as I pressed the reset button before she said anything else.

I hung up and called Bilicia and then Destiny who believed me and asked me the same questions, "What!? By who?"

They didn't even know about my most memorable birthday or about my experience with Markus. Then, like the nurse, they asked, "So what are you going to do?"

No longer crying, but still hurting and confused, I replied, "I don't really know. I guess I have to have an abortion." I had to get rid of this *situation* before it went any further or anyone else found out, but each time I said or even thought about abortion it got harder and harder to accept as my decision. This was going to be the scariest summer of my life.

Lesson Learned:

♥ **The most painful time in my life helped to build my character.** I had looked down on other girls who got pregnant thinking they were just promiscuous and deserved what happened to them. When I found out I was pregnant, I was no different. I was just like any other teenage girl who found herself with child as a child.

A Choice to Make

Even when I walk through the darkest valley, I will not be afraid, for you are close beside me. Your rod and your staff protect and comfort me. -Psalm 23:4

Although my initial response to the nurse was that I would have an abortion, I really didn't know what to do. I experienced every negative emotion a human could feel. Fear, rage, sadness, anxiety, confusion, hate, guilt, and feelings I couldn't even describe consumed my heart and mind daily. Not only did I have those feelings for my current situation, but I felt them in advance for any future decision I might make-confusion if I chose to give the baby up for adoption, guilt for having an abortion, and fear of having the child. How I wished I was considering my options for my first car or a new dress, but instead I was fifteen years old and about to make a grown up decision that I would have to live with for the rest of my life.

Adoption

When I was in middle school, I met a guy about my age who attended a different school. After being friends for a while, he eventually revealed to me that he and his sister were adopted. On the surface, he was a typical teenager who had had a pretty normal life. However, as we got to know each other better, I found out how he really felt. He loved and appreciated his adoptive parents, but he longed to know his natural parents and even felt a sense of abandonment from them. I had heard of other adoption situations and they all seemed to work out for the best interest of the child, but I wasn't convinced that was the best option for me.

As I contemplated the decision before me, I thought about my friend and wondered how my child might feel if I gave it up for adoption. Then I thought about the more immediate situation and realized that I would have to walk around pregnant for nine months just to pass the baby on to someone else. That just didn't make sense to me because the damage to my reputation would have already been done. Everybody would know that I was pregnant. Why would I carry the baby just to give it to somebody else? Adoption just wouldn't work for me.

Abortion

All my life, I thought abortion was wrong. I knew of other people who had abortions, and I disagreed with their decisions to do so. I even looked down on them, but all of that was before I was placed in a situation where abortion seemed to be my best option.

One minute I was doing homework and the next I was researching abortion clinics and methods. No abortion clinics existed in Jackson, and the closest facility was an hour away in Memphis. With my mind made up, I called to make an appointment.

"Hi, um, I would like to make an appointment."

The lady's voice on the other end of the line said, "Okay. How old are you?"

"Um, fifteen."

"Well, I'm gonna need you to have a parent or legal guardian call to make the appointment and to come in with you."

Knowing that I couldn't get that, I hung up the phone frustrated. I didn't know what to do. I had to figure out a way to get rid of the situation without my mother knowing.

I had a cousin who I had been told had an abortion before so I asked my mom if she would take me to visit her. I wanted to ask her what it was like to have an abortion and see if she could help me arrange mine.

When we got to her house, my mother sat in the van while I walked up the six steps to her front door to make sure she was home. When I didn't get an answer at the front, I jumped off the porch and headed to the back door to knock again. I thought, *Maybe jumping off the porch will do the trick, and I won't even have to figure out how to get this abortion.* When I gave up on my cousin answering the door, I returned my mother's van.

She insisted, "You shouldn't be jumping off the porch."

I smirked and asked, "Why?"

The porch wasn't that high off the ground, and I had jumped off of it several times before. She didn't respond. I wondered, *Does she know*?

I didn't talk to my cousin before I took a trip to Washington, D.C. with Chinitra and her family. Shortly after finding out my monthly friend would not be making her regular appearance, I boarded a plane heading to our nation's capitol. Planned long before my new circumstance, this trip was my very first flight and the furthest I had ever been from home. Excited about the trip but plagued by the decision I had to make, I wondered if I would be able to enjoy myself. No one on the trip knew I was pregnant except Chinitra. Sitting next to her in my window seat, I gazed into the clouds wishing I could stay there forever and never return to the ground below.

We finally landed and made our way to our fancy hotel room. Overlooking a plaza where people danced, played, roller bladed, and even uni-cycled both day and night, the window in our room was a retreat for me. I was a little girl with such a grown woman problem. I had always felt mature and everyone, especially my mother, sarcastically called me "grown", but it was at this time in my life that I was slapped into the reality that I was *not* grown.

I was enthralled by the sites in Washington, D.C. and temporarily forgot about being pregnant; however, my body reminded me that there was a foreign substance inside. While touring the White House, I got nauseated and almost collapsed. In a crowd of twenty people on the tour as we stood in the Red Room, I created a seat on the floor to keep from vomiting on the elaborate carpet. When we toured the Capitol, I tilted my head back to look up at the painting on the ceiling and my vision immediately became blurry. Within minutes, I no longer saw the interior of the Capitol or any of the other tourists. I could only see an image similar to the staticy black and white screen seen when a television set goes out. Chinitra helped me to take a seat at the bottom of the staircase in the Capitol. As I embarrassingly sat there as tourists walked past me wondering what was wrong with me, the two adult women on the trip began to get suspicious and probably started to piece together the clues.

Throughout the trip, I snuck away to the pay phone in the lobby of the hotel to call my aunt Pat. Before I left home, we had made a plan for her to set an abortion appointment for me acting as my guardian. I decided abortion was my best option and this approach was my only hope of getting it without my mother knowing.

I nervously dialed Pat's phone number. "Hey, did you do it?"

With hesitation, she sighed, "Yeah, I did it. We'll go next Monday at 9:00 in the morning. I just really hate this whole situation. It's my fault. I'm so sorry, Summer."

"No, Pat. It's my fault. I should have never even stayed in the room with him or let him touch me at all. I knew I didn't like him. I was so stupid."

She made the appointment, but I never made it to the clinic.

Lessons Learned:

- ♥ **Seek mature, Godly advice.** I always wanted to be a grown up and acted "grown", but when faced with a decision, the hardest decision of my life, I was reminded of how much of a child I still was. However, I still was not smart enough to seek advice on my adult decision.

- ♥ **Ignorance is *not* bliss.** Everything I didn't know about sex and pregnancy was exposed. I didn't know about pregnancy prevention, adoption, abortion or having a baby. I had to learn, but I learned the hard way.

The Secret is Revealed

The Lord replied, "Don't say, 'I'm too young,' for you must go wherever I send you and say whatever I tell you.
-Jeremiah 1:7

"God, why me?" Stretched across my bed, I screamed at God for putting me in that situation. Barely having enough energy to cry, the tears continued to soak my pillow. Between my sobs, I heard my mother yell up front from her bedroom. "Summer, can you come here for a second?"

Wiping the tears from my face and trying to calm my eyes and my racing heart, I slowly walked into her room as if nothing was going on and casually said, "Hey Ma, you called me?"

With a concerned look on her face, but not a stern one because she was not a strict person at any time, she asked, "Do you have something you need to tell me?"

"Nooo... Why?" was my response, but she wasn't buying it. She asked again, and my head faced the left wall and the right wall quickly as I shook my head still trying to look normal.

With a hurt look on her face that I had never seen before, she then said, "I was hoping you would be honest with me and just tell me, Summer."

I still played dumb and asked, "Tell you what?" After the back and forth game, she finally told me she had known that I was pregnant for some time.

"Summer, I guess it was my motherly instincts at first because I just knew. Then Junior called and told me he had heard."

The cousin that was with me at the health department had told her aunt and uncle who then told my mother that I was pregnant and planning to have an abortion. On top of all the other emotions I felt, I added betrayal to the list.

This short conversation with my mother ended up being our first and last "sex" talk. After being probed with questions on who, what, how, why, and when, I opened up slightly and told her what had happened to me the morning I turned fifteen. We

34

never had serious conversations as my whole family just liked to make each other laugh, but we were forced to have one then. One of the most awkward moments of my life, I stood before my mother as she outright asked, "Did he penetrate you?"

I didn't know what that meant. All I knew was he got on top of me, I pushed him off of me, and I was then pregnant. I didn't feel anything except the pressure of his body weight on me. I said, "I guess so."

My mother was not a big talker, but she let me know she was completely against abortion, regardless of the circumstances. "Well, Summer, we'll just have to make it work. You can't have an abortion."

I didn't say anything else. I just looked at her coldly as I held back tears and left her bedroom. I heard what she said, but that was not the final word. Knowing my original intentions, my mother kept a close eye on me to make sure I was not sneaking off to Memphis. Once again, I was sick. Not morning sickness though. I was just disgusted that I was being forced to have a baby by someone I did not know.

Although adoption was not what she wanted, my mother suggested it as a compromise between my choice and her demands. "Summer, if you will just let the baby be born, we can bless another family with it. We could even let someone in our family raise it so you could see it."

I tuned her out as she tried to convince me of this option that I had already ruled out. I thought, *If I'm going to have the stigma of being a pregnant teenager, then I might as well keep the baby.*

The problem was that I still did not want to have a baby. I began to think of ways that I could change the situation. When I threatened my mother with my plans to commit suicide, she said she would rather have me and gave in to my demand to have an abortion, but not without a fight. My secret quickly spread as my mother not only told my dad and our pastor that I was pregnant, but also that I was trying to have an abortion and wanted to kill myself. They both called trying to convince me that killing the baby or myself were not solutions, but I didn't want to hear it. I wanted everybody to stop talking to me and to just leave me alone.

My mother ensured that I would not be left alone as she set up meetings and reached out to everyone she knew to pray for me and to fight for her unborn grandchild. She took me to a Planned Parenthood Clinic where they talked to me about abortion and gave me a little plastic fetus to show me how my "baby" looked at that point in my pregnancy. When I got home, I threw the little peach fetus at my bedroom door. I didn't need this visual representation of what I needed to get out of me.

Like my mother, my grandmother didn't say a lot so when I started to get letters from her about how God hated abortion, I felt even more guilt for wanting one. Other family members wrote and made lots of phone calls that I didn't want to take. Holding the phone away from my ear, I feigned listening to whoever was on the other end of the phone line claiming to know what was best for me. One of my grandmother's sisters sent brochures about abortion that showed how the various procedures were done in an attempt to scare me out of doing it. I cried while looking at them and reading the letters, but I still knew what had to be done.

I hated that my mother even knew. For so long, I had been making decisions on my own and doing what I thought was best without much guidance from her or anyone else. Why did this have to be different? When I wanted to take my own life, she agreed to let me have an abortion, but she didn't intend to make it possible for me to do so. I was stubborn and still made another attempt.

With my mother's "consent" for the abortion, my aunt Pat secretly agreed to drive from Bolivar to Jackson to take me to Memphis for the abortion. So that my mother wouldn't see Pat pick me up, I had asked my mother to drop me off at my grandmother's house just to visit. When my mother found out my aunt was on her way to pick me up, she called her insisting that she not come to my grandmother's house. I sat anxiously waiting on my aunt to arrive, but instead I watched as the blue minivan pulled into my grandmother's driveway.

"Pat's not coming, Summer," my mother stated to my back as I headed to my grandmother's bedroom. Following me, she continued, "I'm sorry. I just can't let you do that."

Fury started at my toes and, by the time it reached my mouth, the meanest words I would ever say to my mother shot out like bullets, "I hate you! How could you do this to me? You aren't the one that has to carry a baby by someone you don't know. You won't have to live my life!"

I truly felt that I hated her and that she was ruining my life. She stared at me as I spoke, but she didn't utter a word. That day was the end of my fourteenth week. Since I hadn't made it to Memphis by then, I resigned myself to the fact that I was about to have a baby. My mother left, and I cried myself to sleep in my grandmother's bed while my grandmother let me have the space I desperately needed at that time. I'm sure she was up front praying for me.

Some people asked me where my faith was, and I often asked where my God was. *How did you let this happen to me?* My pastor was a part of my life since before I was baptized. I was certainly a believer in Christ, but I was young in my faith and really, just young. Before I found out I was pregnant, I prayed every night that I wasn't. Once I found out I was pregnant, I prayed it would go away somehow. When my mother decided I couldn't make it go away, I prayed the baby was Markus'. My knees were sore from all the time spent on the side of my bed asking God for what I wanted, but only a few times did I ask for what I really needed-strength and guidance. Lying on the bottom bunk of the set I had shared with Brandy for my entire life, I cried and wished that I could just die so that I would not have to live with the embarrassment of the pregnancy and endure the hard life that would follow. I prayed and prayed, but death seemed like the best way to ease my pain.

It was still very difficult to fathom being pregnant by someone I didn't know, but at least now I was no longer tormented by the decision of whether or not to get an abortion. Although deep down I didn't think the baby was Markus's a part of me held on to the possibility that it could be. Regardless of who the father was, it was official that I was going to be a mother before my sixteenth birthday.

I finally got the nerve to tell Markus I was pregnant, and, not surprisingly, he immediately distanced himself from me saying, "Summer, I know. I already heard, but you know it's not mine."

"Markus, I think it is. You know I'm not sure that *it* really happened with him, but I know it did with you. I know you don't want to be a daddy yet. I don't want to have a baby either, but I have to now. Your mama wants it to be yours too. It'll be okay."

As he shook his head reiterating that he knew the baby growing inside of me was not his, he walked out the front door of his mother's house leaving me sitting there alone until his mother returned home.

Still volunteering at my mother's job, I shared my condition with Susanne, the director of the program. I was working in her office that summer so I spent a lot of time with her. Not knowing what to expect but knowing I had to tell her I was pregnant, I revealed my secret. Susanne simply hugged me and said, "You're such a smart, strong young lady. You and your baby will be just fine. I love you, and I'm here for you. Summer, you'll be a great mother."

Unlike everyone else, she never asked me who the father was. She only cared about me and the child I was carrying. Having six children of her own, Susanne had experienced a lot in her lifetime and made me feel like I was still a good person. She sent me an encouragement card each month of pregnancy and supported me throughout that summer and beyond.

In spite of my pregnancy and depression because of it, I continued to do volunteer work, and I continued to go to church most Sundays when my mother would make yet another trip to Bolivar for the week. Paranoia overcame me in the beginning because I knew everyone knew what had happened to me and were judging me. I wanted to run and hide rather than continue going to church as the women of the church frowned with disappointment with me as they pulled their "sweet" daughters away from me. It no longer mattered that I made good grades, did volunteer work and was very active in school. I had become just another pregnant teenage girl and a poor role model. Many people inside and outside of the church ostracized me, but Pastor Hammond embraced me through it all and told me I was still a good person.

Although I was young, I had pictured my life long before I got pregnant and this wasn't in it. After I finished college and got a great job, my handsome husband and I would start our family. We would be happily married, and our children would love me and respect me as their mother, and they would know and love their biological father who was in the house with us every day. Experiencing the challenges of being a stepchild, I knew my perfect little family would have to consist of my husband and me and our children together. I would not subject my children to a stepfather who had to adjust and try to love a child who was not his as much as he loved his own, and I would not put my husband in a position to have to fight for my attention either.

For me, being a stepchild meant not knowing exactly where I belonged. In my household in Jackson, I was the only person out of seven with my last name, which was my mother's maiden name. Everyone else had my stepfather's name. In Nashville my dad and his wife had his last name. I was Summer Owens. No one made a point to make me feel different, but I did. I knew my parents and siblings loved me, but I always felt like I was alone and never fully a part of either family. My children wouldn't have that. They would never feel like they were forcing their parents to make a choice between them and their spouse. My children would never have to face each holiday choosing which family they would spend it with and worry about hurting the other's feelings.

Nope. I knew I would do it all right by having children *after* I got married so that I wouldn't have to worry about any of those things. Wrong. Because I had been violated and was now pregnant by a stranger, if I ever wanted a husband, my child would be someone's stepchild. Not only that, my child wouldn't have to worry about splitting holidays with parents because he wouldn't even know his father and would spend holidays only with me and my family. He would not have a daddy at all. It was just me - his fifteen year old mother, but I did not want to be or feel like his sister as some suggested. I was carrying this baby. I would be the one to push him out, and I would be the one who got to be called "Mama".

In that moment, I remembered a scene that had played out only months earlier. *No, that wouldn't happen to me,* I thought to myself as I nervously entered the third floor hospital room where my cousin rested on the bed ten months before her fifteenth birthday and three months before mine. The third floor was the maternity floor, and she had just given birth six months into her pregnancy. Our family filled the tiny hospital room. The mother and sister of the baby's father were there too and even brought a package of pampers, but the father was nowhere to be found. As I sat in a chair next to my young cousin's hospital bed, I looked at her thinking about the baby dolls we had put away only a couple of years earlier and how she then had a real one. Scanning the room I confirmed that the boy who had gotten my cousin pregnant still was not present and would not be. Picturing myself in a hospital bed, I thought to myself, *This is crazy. I would never let anything like this happen to me.* The very next February when I was fifteen years old, I was laying in a hospital bed on the third floor of the same hospital holding my own baby.

Lessons Learned:

♥ **Focus on the future.** It doesn't matter how the pregnancy happened. The end result is a live baby that needs love, attention, and support. I couldn't dwell on how my baby was conceived.

♥ **We don't always get our way, and that's a good thing.** I wasn't ready to be a mother, and if I had my way, I wouldn't have been yet. However, my mother insisted that I accept responsibility for the baby growing inside of me. Had she not, I would have lived with the regret of having an abortion, and I would have missed out on the blessings that came from my child.

♥ **Have faith in God.** At times, I didn't really know or see God. I was hurting. I was embarrassed. I was confused. I felt like a failure. People talked about me. I was sick and depressed. However, God had a plan and a purpose for all that I went through.

♥ **Never say never.** As soon as I said I would never end up pregnant as a teenager, I did. I had my life all figured out, and it did not include the stigma and challenges of being a teenage mother.

The Pregnant, Little Girl

This is my command—be strong and courageous! Do not be afraid or discouraged. For the Lord your God is with you wherever you go. -Joshua 1:9

As the weeks went by and I began to accept the inevitable truth that I was going to be a teenage mother, my mother set my first doctor's appointment. Walking into the cold doctor's office my palms began to sweat and my heart began to race as I speculated, *What would they have to do to me? Will I have take off all my clothes? Will they just touch my stomach?* Dr. Rogers reached for my hand, greeting me as my mother and I entered the examination room, "Hi, Summer. We're just gonna check everything out and make sure you and the baby are doing okay. Alright?"

Still not knowing what to expect next, I tensely responded, "Okay," and waited for further instructions. I think my mother had already told her my age and that I had never been examined by a gynecologist. And at my first visit, she was also serving in the role as my obstetrician. The closest thing I had experienced to a gynecologist visit was the health department, and then I only urinated in a cup. Maybe if I hadn't gone into shock when that nurse told me I was pregnant, I would have experienced an examination that day and would have known what to expect then.

"Okay, Summer. I need you to disrobe from the waist down and place this across your lap once you sit back on the table," the doctor instructed as she handed me a sheet made from the same material as hospital gowns.

She and my mother left the room, and I hesitantly began to pull down my jeans. Once I was safely back on the examination table, the doctor returned to the room and instructed me to lay back and place my feet in the stirrups. I placed one foot in each holder on either side of the table, but my knees insisted on kissing.

Laughing a little, Dr. Rogers said, "You're gonna have to open your legs and slide your bottom down so we can make sure everything is okay."

I thought, *No, there is no way I'm going to lay on this table with my legs spread apart for you to see. No, we'll have to come up with another way. You're lucky I pulled my pants off!* Her fake half-smile told me there was no compromise so I surrendered. Leaning back on my elbows and scooting my bare bottom down to the edge of the table knees pointing at opposite walls, I thought the hard part was over. Wrong.

"Okay, Summer. You're going to feel a little discomfort," she said as she jammed what I later learned was called a speculum up my vagina headed for my brain. Cringing with pain, not discomfort, I thought, *Well, I'm definitely not a virgin now.*

She asked, "You okay?" as I lay on my back eyes closed tightly.

I released the breath I had been holding to whimper, "I guess."

After the dreadful Pap smear, I got dressed and followed a nurse to a room where I got to see and hear the baby inside of me. As my mother and I walked down the hall, I glimpsed at her and was thankful to have such a supportive mother. Later as the nurse slid the ultra sound machine across the cold gel on my only slightly larger than normal stomach, she smiled as she explained what we were seeing on the monitor, "Well, that's the head, and those are the arms and legs. Can you see she's sucking her thumb? Yes, I believe we have a little girl."

As I looked at the tiny skeleton on the screen, I pictured my little girl thinking, *Would she look like me?* The nurse continued explaining the quick "whop, whop" sound coming from the machine. "Your baby's heartbeat sounds normal. So far so good."

Although she smiled at me and I even half-smiled back at her, guilt quickly set in as I thought, *I can't believe that I was trying so hard to get rid of this little heartbeat. This little face.* Up to that point, "you're pregnant" had just been a phrase people used to describe my condition, but from that moment on "I'm pregnant" was a reality I could finally accept. There was a real, live baby inside of me. However, accepting the fact that I was pregnant didn't make it any less frightening.

I tried to rationalize, *I am really about to have a baby. How I am going to do this? How will this baby look? What if she looks like him? How will I look at her? Oh God, what have I gotten myself into? Wait a minute, maybe the baby is Markus' and will look like him. But thank God it's a girl. I'll be raising this baby without a father and surely God wouldn't give me a boy to raise alone. I had already been punished enough.* Finally escaping my own thoughts, I left the doctor's office and went home with my mother.

In addition to going to the doctor, my mother took me to the health department to find out if I qualified for the WIC (Women Infants and Children) food program. A form of public assistance, the WIC program was designed to help ensure pregnant mothers had access to nutritious food for themselves and their unborn babies. From milk and cereal to cheese and juice, WIC foods were a major part of my diet and provided me with the help we needed on groceries. To use WIC, I had a voucher that I submitted at the cash register. Sometimes I was embarrassed, but this experience humbled me. I needed WIC and so did my baby. WIC was a blessing but not a crutch as I did not want to allow myself to always depend on public assistance. I used WIC to meet my needs until I could do better on my own.

My entire pregnancy was a giant roller coaster with so many dips and curves that I couldn't tell if I was nauseous from the pregnancy or the emotional roller coaster ride. From the moment I found out I was pregnant, I experienced shame, denial, shock, fear, anger, hurt, confusion, depression, and loneliness. On any given day, I could feel every one of those emotions. But time didn't wait for me to reconcile my feelings before I had to return to school and face my classmates.

That August, I started my tenth grade year of high school. Entering my third month of pregnancy, I still looked normal. However, by the time I stepped foot on the bus the first day of school almost everyone already knew what I thought was my secret. Hiding behind the smile I always wore on my face, I ignored questions that morning and for as long as possible refusing to deal with the situation or discuss what had happened to me or the embarrassment of being pregnant. I figured I would surrender my Fifth Amendment right once I was showing and could no longer deny that I was pregnant.

Getting adjusted to my changing body and at the same time sitting through classes with morning sickness was a challenge. As my baby began to grow, I got more unwanted attention and could no longer deny my pregnancy. The good thing was that I no longer got the question, "Are you pregnant?" because it was obvious that I was. My sister, Brandy, even told me that our seven-year-old brother, Stephen, asked her, "Why is Summer getting so fat?" He didn't know I was pregnant, but everyone else did. However, I began to get a much harder question, "But who is the father?" My last boyfriend didn't go to my school so not many people knew about him and no one really ever saw me with anyone. I think everyone from teachers to students to church members and even strangers wanted to know. I usually responded with, "Oh, you don't know him," or "He doesn't live here." Those were true statements. I didn't even know him. However, I openly hoped and prayed that my ex-boyfriend, Markus, was my unborn baby's father.

Not only did I care deeply for Markus, but I loved his mother, Kaye. She loved me too. Throughout my pregnancy, I talked to Kaye often. After my doctor's appointments, I usually didn't return to school that day. In the same hot minivan we drove to and from Bolivar each day when I was volunteering, my mother and I did the same after my doctor's appointments. Although I didn't have my license yet, my mother would let me drop her off at work so that I could drive to Kaye's house ten minutes away. During the day, Markus was at school, but Kaye worked from home so she was almost always home after my appointments. Whenever someone would come to her house while I was there, she would introduce me as her daughter and point to my stomach saying with a smile, "That's my grandbaby right there."

She and I both knew that it was a possibility that the baby inside of me was not Markus's, but she always said it didn't matter because I was her daughter and my baby would be her grandbaby. Kaye always spoke highly of me and was very encouraging like Susanne, and she always made me feel so good about how I was managing my schoolwork, extra curricular activities, pregnancy, sickness, and doctor's appointments. "Summer, it's gonna be okay. You just keep hanging in there and you and my grandbaby will be just fine." Enjoying her company, conversation, and confirmation, I would sit with Kaye until my mother got off work.

That year, I was on the Jackson Central-Merry High School yearbook staff, as well as other student organizations. Throughout my pregnancy, I was determined to stay true to myself and be the same person I would have been before the pregnancy. It was challenging, but I did it and did not quit any of my commitments. I was thankful for the wonderful mother-figures God had placed in my life, and I was especially blessed to have a great mother and her support of all that I was doing.

Although mostly quiet with few words of encouragement, my own mother was my number one supporter and took me to all of my doctor's appointments. She was by my side for each and every one of them without question or complaint, and I was thankful for that. A mix of emotions filled me daily, but at times the positive ones won the fight for my mind. Often scared because with each visit I came closer to being a mother, I also grew excited about seeing the little person growing inside of me. My mother's presence helped to keep me balanced. However, I always wondered how it would feel to have the father of my baby with me. I didn't actually want my baby's father because of what had happened, but I often imagined having a loving husband at the appointments with me instead of or along with my mother. My mother did all she could, but she just couldn't be who she wasn't. She wasn't the father, and it wasn't her fault.

Lessons Learned:

♥ **Recognize and appreciate support.** I didn't do it nearly enough. I should have thanked my mother for taking so much time away from her job to take me to the doctor. There were so many other people that I should have shown more appreciation for even if it was with a simple gesture.

♥ **Public assistance can be a friend and an enemy.** Used properly, public assistance can help people survive in a period in their lives when government assistance is needed. Too often, people get comfortable with the limiting lifestyle public assistance provides and don't strive for independence from the system and impose a life of poverty on themselves and their children.

Thank God for Friends

Two people are better off than one, for they can help each other succeed. If one person falls, the other can reach out and help. But someone who falls alone is in real trouble.
-Ecclesiastes 4:9-10 NIV

I had a great group of friends who supported me throughout my entire pregnancy. Even though I often felt alone even in a room full of people, I usually had someone to talk to or cry with when I was down. One of my friends even supplied all the pants for my maternity wardrobe. Never investing in maternity clothes, I cycled through the five pairs of jeans my friend had given me because they were too big for her. Pushing a rubber band through the button hole and wrapping it around the metal button on the jeans, I transformed the jeans into maternity pants. Extra large shirts purchased at Wal-mart completed my set of maternity clothes and got me through my pregnancy.

During my eighth month of pregnancy, one evening my friend Shannon picked me up to visit another friend named Cynthia at her house as we often did. When we pulled into the driveway, I got a strange feeling that was confirmed when I walked through the door. "Surprise!" a room full of my friends and family screamed and hugged me as I proceeded to the living room with my hands covering my mouth still open from both shock and happiness.

Directed to a plush, velvet chair decorated with pink and blue streamers, I waddled across the room and then rested. Sitting there I beamed as I scanned the room full of people who cared about me. From my mother and grandmother to long-time and new friends, I was relieved to see how far we'd come. In that room I felt safe. No one was judging me and no one made me feel like a failure. They were supporting me in every way they could. I couldn't believe my friends were having a baby shower for me because we were all still broke little girls. None of us had jobs yet. I wondered as I scanned the room, *How did they get the money to put this together?*

We played a few games, ate, and then, "Open your gifts!" the room later excitedly expressed sounding even more anxious to see the gifts than I was. Tearing away all the wrapping paper, I couldn't believe the great gifts I had gotten from my young friends. Still resting inside of me, my baby was all set with a new stroller, a baby carrier, diapers, clothes, bottles, bibs, and more. The tears that rolled down my fat cheeks were caught by the big shirt that covered the bubble that held my baby.

After the baby shower, I didn't think I would end up back at Cynthia's house again so soon though. Being a stubborn child, I had never had the best relationship with my stepfather. However, things got worse while I was pregnant. Like any parent, he wasn't proud that his teenage daughter was pregnant. I was already a strong-willed and emotional teenager, and I'm sure my escalating hormones only heightened the tension.

One cool, fall afternoon while I was preparing for a day away from the house, it all came to a head. After setting up the ironing board in front of the sink of our small kitchen, I headed to my bedroom to pick out my clothes for a visit with my friend's mother at her sewing shop. After I didn't return to the ironing board after a few minutes, my stepfather got upset that the ironing board was in the way and demanded I put it up. Because I hadn't ironed my clothes yet, I refused. I was almost finished picking out my clothes and was nearly ready to iron so it didn't make sense to put it up just to take it right back out. When I ignored his order to put it up, he told me I couldn't go with my friend. When she arrived to pick me up, I was ordered to stay in the house while he went outside to tell her I could no longer go.

My mother wasn't there to intercede. I don't know if she would have or not, but he put the ironing board up himself as I cried in my bedroom and decided I no longer wanted to live in that house. With only the clothes on my back, I stormed out of the house without a destination at first. Soon after I left, the afternoon was behind me and the sun had begun to set. Not noticing when I left, my stepfather didn't know I was gone and my mother still hadn't returned. Afraid but upset, I marched down my street looking over my shoulder for either my stepfather or my mother to pull up behind me.

Still looking back, I passed Chinitra's house then Destiny's house because I knew my mom would look for me there first. The little sun that was out when I started walking quickly hid as soon as I turned on the next street forcing me to walk down the longest street with tall, scary trees that leaned into the street with branches and leaves hovering over me in the dark. The mean trees finally released me, and I made it to the main street which at least had a couple of street lights and some traffic.

I kept walking until I got to Cynthia's house a few blocks away. When I arrived, I acted like I was just paying her a casual visit, "Hey, Cynthia. I just thought I'd stop by. What you doing?"

She responded with a puzzled look, "Nothing. Come in," as she peered out the door behind me trying to figure out how I got there. I didn't want Cynthia or her parents to notify my mother that I had run away to their house so I just sat and talked to my friend, but our conversation didn't last long.

Cynthia's phone rang, and she answered, "Hello..."

Looking at me she then said, "Yeah, she's right here."

As I had figured, my mother started her search efforts with Chinitra and Destiny who lived in our neighborhood. When she found out that I wasn't with them, she put them to work and they found me at Cynthia's house. That night my mother picked me up and took me to my grandmother's house because I did not want to go back to the house with my stepfather. Returning to my mother's house to get my few belongings, I moved in permanently with my grandmother.

With a quiet demeanor much like my mother's, my grandmother embraced me and my unborn baby without saying anything about the fact that I had run away. Because serious conversations were difficult for my family, challenging issues were often dealt with through written communication. I fully expected to get a letter from my grandmother about me leaving home and living with her, but I never did. She lived only about ten minutes away from my mother and around the corner from my friend Shannon so I rode to school with Shannon.

We continued that routine until February 3, 1995. I had decided that would be my last day of school because my baby was due on February 15th, and I couldn't endure walking back and forth across the long crosswalk every day. At the end of each class on my last day, I told each teacher that I was going to be out until after my baby was born and that someone from the home schooling program would contact them about getting my schoolwork. Although I had not yet contacted the department of education to request a home school teacher, I figured the process would be simple and I could get a teacher for the following Monday. Because I was so strong-willed and independent, my mother almost always took a step back and just let me do whatever I thought was best as was the case with home schooling. I told everyone goodbye that Friday afternoon with the expectation that the next time I would see them would be after I had my baby. When I got home from school, I called the department of education. I explained my situation to them and requested a home school teacher starting Monday.

The receptionist asked, "Okay. Have you had the baby?"

"No, but I'm due in two weeks."

"Well, we can't assign you a teacher until you have delivered the baby. You'll just have to go to school until then."

I immediately thought, *There's no way I'm going back to school now that I've told everyone that was my last day!*

Although I was not calm, I politely whined, "But I can't. I can't walk across the crosswalk and carry all those heavy books for two more weeks."

She jokingly responded, "You never know; you might have the baby tonight."

I wasn't amused by her humor and was upset that I would have to return to school; or so I thought.

Lessons Learned:

- ♥ **Thank God for friends.** My friends supported me and even took time and money they did not have to spare to throw me a shower. Although that was one big gesture, many small gestures made me appreciate the love and support I had from them when I needed them most.

- ♥ **Thank God for parents and grandparents.** The love and support of my family got me through my pregnancy.

- ♥ **I could run away from home, but I couldn't run away from my problems.** Even though I left my mother and stepfather's house, I was still pregnant and would have to deal with being a teenage mother no matter where I lived.

A Child is Born

A woman when she is in travail hath sorrow, because her hour is come: but as soon as she is delivered of the child, she remembereth no more the anguish, for joy that a man is born into the world. -John 16:21

Later that night, I braced myself on the edge of the kitchen table as I headed down the hall to my grandmother's bedroom. I hunched over from the pain in my stomach. I wondered, *Are these cramps or could they be contractions? Is the baby coming early?*

I didn't know what to expect when the time came so I called my mother, "Mama, I'm having real bad cramps. Do you think the baby is coming?"

Calm as always, she replied, "I don't know. Is it one cramp that won't go away or are they coming and going?"

"Um, it stops hurting for a minute then it hurts again."

"Okay, I'll ask Dr. Rodgers." After only a few minutes, she called me back, "Okay. She believes you're having contractions, and she wants you to come in if they are less than five minutes apart."

Just in case I would be going to the hospital that night, I decided to take a shower to stall for time to ensure it was really time before heading to the hospital. Holding onto the wet tile of the shower walls when the contractions hit, I survived the shower. With contractions coming every few minutes, I eased out of the tub and maneuvered into a two-piece salmon pink, cotton pants set someone had given my mom. I looked like a big, fat pig, but the rubber-banded jeans wouldn't work for that trip. I called my mother, and she rushed to my grandmother's house and took me to the hospital to deliver my baby. It looked like the lady at the department of education was right. My heart raced with my thoughts as my mother sped to the hospital. I was scared, but I was tired of carrying the basketball inside of me.

Lying in the hospital bed, I clinched my fists and grimaced through each contraction and thanked God for the few minutes of relief between them. Hooked up to a machine that displayed my contractions, as well as the baby's heartbeat, I felt the contractions in my body and watched them on the monitor too. As the nurse prepared me for delivery, she began to put an IV in my arm. In her attempt to do so, she punctured a vein in my right arm and blood shot everywhere.

My warm blood ran down my skinny arm and sprayed everything on and around me. There was so much blood that the clumsy nurse had to change my once pale blue gown and white sheets on the long, narrow hospital bed. My heart nearly beat out of my chest. I was fifteen years old about to somehow push a huge basketball out of a small hole in my body. The nurse cleaned the blood, and when my heart stopped racing I realized I had forgotten about the contractions that only minutes before had crippled me. Panicking from the pain of the needle and then seeing my blood all over the place made me forget everything. However, once the IV was safely in my arm and the blood was cleaned up I remembered the contractions and felt the pain again.

Lying in a pool of wetness after the nurse inserted a long, thin object inside of me bursting the fluid sack that surrounded my baby, I prayed for the painful ordeal to end. When I thought I couldn't endure any longer, the nurses helped me into a sitting position. "Okay, be real still," the nurse instructed me as she prepared to administer the epidural. As I arched my back and gripped the bed rail, she pierced the small of my back with the long needle. Conflicting feelings of fear from seeing the needle and the need for pain relief were resolved without my feedback and I was helped back onto my pillow. As my lower body began to go numb and I no longer felt the pain from the contractions, I was relieved that the needle won the fight. My legs quickly began to get numb and heavy. Soon all sensation left my body from the waist down, and my left leg preferred the side of my hospital bed as it kept sliding off of it. Every time it did, I asked my mother to lift it back onto the bed because I simply could no longer maneuver the huge piece of lead that my leg had become.

Always calm or perhaps just hiding her truly feelings, my mother manned a post at my head. Standing and sometimes sitting by my side, she provided a few words of comfort but was mostly quiet crocheting or watching television until the main event began. "It'll be over before you know it," she said with a half smile that held back tears.

Somewhat ashamed to look at her, I knew she was thinking, *I just can't believe we're here. My baby is having a baby, and she's still a baby. How are we going to do this? I have children at home already and now another one. How did this happen to us?* Although I was sad that I had disappointed my mother, my own physical pain overrode any emotional pain she or I felt at the time. The stirrups felt like ice chips pressed against the ashy soles of my tiny feet, but that was nothing compared to the crippling pain at the foot of my belly.

The doctor came in regularly to check my dilation by sticking her fingers deep inside of me. The last time she checked, I was nine centimeters dilated which meant it was time for me to start pushing. I clinched the bedrails and started to push trying to get this thing that had been growing inside of me out of my body. Through my knees spread as wide as an eagle's wings, I saw my doctor's head as she reached inside of my vagina in an attempt to pull the baby down.

"We can't see the head yet. The baby's actually turned sideways," she calmly stated as she insisted that I keep pushing while she tried to reposition the baby to come down the birth canal. "Come on, Summer. Give us a big one now."

"Ugggghhhh!" I grunted again as I pushed as hard as I could for less than a minute but I couldn't give her anymore before taking a break.

When my eyes weren't on the doctor seated between my legs or on my mother by my head, they were on the small, round clock on the wall behind her. I watched the clock beginning at 1:00 AM and wondered how long this could possibly take. I thought, *Is this ever going to end? Can I just give up? Just leave it alone. It's not coming out.* I was so tired and saw no progress being made.

After an hour of grunting and pushing, my doctor broke the news to me, "Summer, this baby's stubborn. We're going to have to perform a C-section."

My heart stalled as the reality of what she said sank in. A C-section meant they were going to cut my stomach open to get the baby out. My mother had endured three C-sections, and I was thankful she was there to comfort me; but I was still scared. It was me who was going to be cut this time. Before I could turn my head to show my mother my frightened face, I was being whisked away to the operating room.

Once in the operating room, a nurse administered a different anesthesia in preparation for the surgery. They then strapped my arms down, put an oxygen mask over my mouth and nose, and placed a blue sheet vertically above my stomach so that I couldn't watch as they cut me open. I began to panic again when the oxygen mask started to smother me.

Because my mouth was covered, I tried to tell my mother with my eyes that I couldn't breathe. She was sitting in a chair by my head, and eventually could see that I thought I was going to die-not from childbirth but from the oxygen! However, she didn't take the mask off my mouth. For a very short period of time, she rubbed my head and said all she knew to say, "Well, Summer. It will be okay. It'll be over before you know it." She probably had a million thoughts and emotions, but I would never know them.

So focused on trying to breathe with the oxygen mask that was smothering me, I almost didn't feel the pressure of the knife as the doctor began to cut through the layers of my abdomen. Closing my eyes and praying it would be over soon, I felt helpless and just hoped I wouldn't die. The doctors and nurses didn't share the same concern and spent the entire time discussing a party they had attended the previous weekend. "Yes, Tricia was there, and the food was great," one nurse chatted. I thought to myself, *Are you kidding me? Could you please concentrate on what you are doing?*

At 2:24 AM, nearly an hour and half after I started pushing, a healthy baby was removed from my body. Transferring the baby to my mother who still sat at my head, the doctor announced, "It's a boy!"

The oxygen mask continued to stifle my speech as I thought, *What? I was supposed to have a girl. After my ultrasound early in my pregnancy, my doctor told me I was having a girl. All the superstitious people said I was having a girl because of how my stomach sat. There was no father for the baby so it had to be a girl. How was I going to raise a boy by myself? Although it would still be hard, I could handle a girl. I'm a girl so I know how to be a girl, but I do not know how to be a boy or raise a boy. Someone must have made a mistake.*

I couldn't even bring myself to look at the baby in my mother's arms. Trying to fathom how I ended up with a boy, I remained stuck on my back eyes closed tightly imagining my future with a little boy and wanted the doctor to quickly sew me up. Like with the incision, I felt the pressure of each stitch and wanted them to concentrate more. However, they picked right back up on the party conversation that they paused earlier just to say, "It's a boy."

I finally got the nerve to look over at my baby after my mother said, "Look at him, Summer. He's so sweet."

I didn't say a word as I turned my head on my pillow to face them. He was beautiful. I was amazed and even surprised by his fair skin and thick, silky black hair. His hair covered every spot on his tiny head. After taking in the miracle before me, my next feeling was thankfulness. Not only was my baby beautiful and healthy, but he also didn't look like the boy who forced himself on me. In fact he looked like Markus's father, and I believed that God had answered my prayer of making the baby Markus's.

The nurses rolled me into the recovery room shivering like I was naked at the North Pole. Explaining that I was cold because I had been opened up, the nurses reassured me that I would be comfortable soon. After my shivering calmed down, the nurses moved me out of recovery and into a hospital room.

All of my young friends filled the room along with my family. Susanne was there too. Markus and his mother Kaye arrived in the midst of the commotion. They agreed that my baby looked like Markus' father, and I believed that they wanted my baby to be theirs too. Everyone coddled him, and I watched as I continued to tremble. "Summer, he's so cute," and "Can I hold him?" were the words I heard over and over again. Still wrapped tightly from head to toe in warm blankets, I could barely move and was still too tired to even talk so I responded with a slight nod and an exhausted smile.

I rested on the bed scanning my hospital room with all of its guests. Friends and family filled the room at that moment and others would flow in and out during my visit. Sure, everyone was excited about seeing the new baby, but I began to wonder about the future. *How many of my friends will still be my friends a few years from now? Will anyone help me take care of this baby? What about when he gets older? Will any of these people still care when he's no longer a cute newborn baby? I can't believe I just did it. I just had a baby. What's next? How am I going to do this?*

I was a mother, and I had a *son.* I thought I would have a daughter, and her name would be Jasmine. Although I had just given birth to a little boy, I had not even considered boy names during my pregnancy.   Asking my friends and family for suggestions, I finally got a recommendation, "Name him Jaylan!" Unique at the time, the name sounded nice to me and I decided to make it official. For his middle name, I honored my father by giving him his middle name of Nathaniel knowing that my father would be the closest person my son would have to an actual father. Adding his name and completing the paperwork for my new baby's birth certificate, I put my lone signature on the document. I was the one and only parent.

Still fighting through abdominal pain, my time in the hospital ended way too early. After only two days, I was heading home with my baby. Helped into a wheelchair because I couldn't walk on my own, I was pushed to my mother's snow-covered minivan parked in the loading area in front of the hospital. Holding my baby dressed in a thick blue hooded jumpsuit and wrapped in blankets, I braced myself for the cold outside and for the struggle ahead of us. Flurries of snow continued to fall on the cold February morning as my mother placed her grandson in his car seat and helped me out of my wheelchair and into the van. I thought, *Here we go, kid. Let's see if we can do this,* as we headed to my home at my grandmother's house to begin our new lives together.

Lessons Learned:

♥ **Having babies is for grownups.** The entire ordeal was painful and scary, and I just wasn't mature enough to emotionally deal with it.

♥ **Once a teenager has a baby, they can no longer be the child.** It's time to grow up. I had always felt and acted mature for my age, but once I had a child I felt like a child with a responsibility I was not ready to handle but knew I no longer had a choice.

No Time to Look Back

No, dear brothers and sisters, I have not achieved it, but I focus on this one thing: Forgetting the past and looking forward to what lies ahead. -Philippians 3:13

Through a thick blanket of snow, my mother drove me and her very first grandchild to my grandmother's house. At the end of the short drive from the hospital, the snow continued to fall as we made our way into the house. In one hand, my mother held the carrier with my new baby, and I held on to her other arm stumbling and hunched over holding my stomach still in pain from the C-section.

As we made it to the door, my beautiful, seventy-three-year-old grandmother stood bracing herself on the wall with one hand and rubbing her long, silver-gray hair with the other. She welcomed us home with a soft hug and slowly stated with a little laugh behind her words, "Well, looks like you brought the baby and the snow home witcha," as she leaned over lovingly hitting my mother as she laughed at her own joke. Still protecting my stitches, I giggled and so did my mother as we headed to the back of the house to my grandmother's bedroom.

I placed my baby in an old, off-white bassinette that my mother had set up next to my grandmother's queen-sized bed. I had been sharing a bed with my grandmother since I moved in, and the bassinette was located where I could easily get to my baby. Although my grandmother had two extra bedrooms, they were both filled with old furniture, clothes, newspapers and other items that could probably have been disposed of if she would have allowed it.

When we got home, we left a few things in the living room as we rested in the back bedroom. One of them was a baby Mickey Mouse balloon that read "It's a Boy!" Mysteriously hovering over my baby, that balloon always ended up wherever he slept. Whether Jaylan was in the bassinette, in my grandmother's bed, or in the front room on the couch, without us even noticing the balloon moving, it would be near him. The explanation my grandmother provided was that my grandfather's spirit was watching over my baby, "That's Kirk looking at his new great-grandbaby. Ha!" my grandmother said with a laugh.

When the physical pain of giving birth finally began to subside, my emotional pain began to set in again. Looking at my son lying on the bed so sweet and peaceful sent daggers through my heart. Hearing his cries sent chills down my spine because all he had was me. He was a baby boy without a father and perhaps he would always be a little boy without a father. And eventually, he would be a teenager and a man without a father. All he had was a mother who was still a child herself, a grandmother who had five children of her own, a grandfather who lived hours away, and a sweet great-grandmother who loved him. He had my dad's family too, but they just weren't close enough either. He had lots of people who loved him, but who would help him learn to be a boy and then show him how to be a man? None of us could be his father. Most days during my maternity leave from school, I would just hold him as I cried because it was all my fault that he was fatherless. He didn't ask to be here, and I didn't know what to do.

Other days, sometimes out of my own guilt and sometimes out of frustration, I couldn't stand to look at him. My whole life was different. His life would be horrible and so would mine. No, it wasn't his fault. Even though I often blamed myself, it really wasn't my fault either.

Sometimes I asked my grandmother to tend to him in her room in the back while I secretly cried myself to sleep on the couch in her living room. She spent most of her time in her bedroom so the front of the house was my space-the place where I could be to myself to release the tears that were constantly putting pressure on my heart. Words came out too. I cried out to God screaming, *Why me?! I know I'm stubborn and don't always respect my parents like I should, but I'm not that bad. I'm really a good kid. I work hard. I'm a good student. I had dreams. I had goals. I had so much I wanted to do with my life. I'm a Christian, and I was a virgin until that happened. Why me, Lord?*

I wept every day of the six weeks I was out of school, but over time I learned the answer to the question I posed to God, *Lord, why would you give me a child by a man I don't know and when I'm nowhere near ready to be mother? Why does my life have to be messed up now? And if you just had to make me have a baby, why on earth couldn't I at least have a girl so I would know what to do a little bit?*

God revealed to me that He wanted me to raise a man unlike any other man I had encountered. My son would be the intelligent, handsome, chivalrous, and God-fearing man I had seen so few of in my life. He wanted me to be an example for another young girl showing her she could thrive as a teenage mother too. I learned that sometimes we don't understand the pain and the heartache, but when I got more mature I knew that it always meant that God was using me. All the tears I shed could have filled a river, but I decided that my tears would not be shed in vain.

Still dealing with the pain in my sewn-up abdomen and my heavy heart, I began home schooling. Unpleasantly surprised on my first day, I met my home school teacher. I heard her car pull up to the curb, as she arrived at my grandmother's house. With my left hand protecting my stitches, I unlocked and opened the wooden door then the iron door and finally the screen door in my grandmother's living room using my one free hand. Observing the heavy-set lady who walked with a limp, I figured she was probably in her late fifties. Still having only one free hand, I helped her get inside the house as she struggled with the four small steps outside the front door. Pulling her up the stairs certainly did not help my healing process.

When she got inside, she introduced herself, "Hi, Summer, right?" I nodded still in a little pain from helping her inside. "Thanks for helping me inside. This leg has given me trouble for some time. I'm Mrs. Tally, and I'll be your home school teacher."

Next, she opened up her bag and took out a few worksheets from a couple of my classes and said she would bring more on her next visit. Looking over a list of my class subjects, Geometry, French II, and Chemistry among others, and shaking her head she uttered, "I can bring you the worksheets each week when I come, but I can't help you with the work. Do you have someone who might be able to help you complete them?"

With a smile of disbelief I responded, "I guess I'll figure it out."

For the next six weeks she brought me worksheets once a week, and I did my best to teach myself what everyone else was learning from the teachers in class. The entire time I was thinking, *Lady, did you see my subjects? How am I supposed to teach myself these subjects?*

As I completed the worksheets, I also began to not only accept, but embrace, the fact that I was a mother. I began to look for ways to gain my independence back and even the self-confidence I had just begun to feel before getting pregnant. I wanted to be excited about my future again.

When one of my mother's co-workers gave her an old, full-sized bed and mattress that her family no longer needed, my mother gave it to me and I knew it was finally time for me to have a room of my own in my grandmother's house. One of the bedrooms in the front of the house had an attached bathroom so I asked my grandmother if I could make that one my room. I spent the next week sifting through all the stuff in that room, either moving it into the other spare bedroom or throwing it away. On an old radio that my dad had given me for my birthday a few years earlier, I listened to my favorite cassette that got me inspired to get my act together both in my room and in my life. It was Chantay Savage's song "I Will Survive".

As she and I sang, "I used to cry, but now I hold my head up high," I pulled out the big, plastic comforter bag where I kept all the clothes I had received for Jaylan at my baby shower or that my mother had bought. I sorted them by size placing them in the drawers I had designated for him in an old chest of drawers. There were a few sleepers and gowns, a few cute, typical baby boy outfits with dogs and trains and balls, and then there were the jogging suits which were the staples of my baby's wardrobe. Finding a great deal on baby jogging suits, my mother racked up getting them in all sizes and all colors. I was never the superficial type who needed to dress my baby in name brands or fancy clothes all the time. I was fifteen years old with a baby, without a father for him and without a job. My baby just needed good, clean clothes.

Thankfully, my WIC had begun to cover baby formula and eventually baby cereal so my baby was fed, and I had a little money in my savings account. Since my dad had been paying my mother child support, she had given me most of the money which I always put into a savings account and used to buy gifts for people and things I needed for school. The balance was never very high. Using the little money left in my savings account, I splurged and bought a new comforter set to decorate my new bedroom. The bed my mother had been given was very old and even falling apart in places, but it was mine. I'd always slept in a twin bed other than when I slept with my grandmother, and now I had my very own full-size bed. As I put the bed skirt on my bed and shams on the pillows, I felt an overwhelming since of pride and accomplishment. I looked at my baby who was staring at me as he moved back and forth in his baby swing in our new bedroom and said with tears in my eyes and hope in my heart, *Baby, I don't know how I'm going to do it, but we'll be okay...I guess.*

That room became my haven and was much better than my cry couch. Although it only had a folding screen as a door, when I pull it together I could close myself and my baby off from the world that had been so cruel to me I thought.

I fell in love with my new bed too. First of all, because it was mine. However, as I began to sleep in it with my baby, I gained a new appreciation for it. The headboard had cutout spaces like a bookshelf where I kept a bottle, pampers and baby wipes so that I didn't have to get out of the bed two or three times a night to quiet my baby's tears. He was right beside me and so was everything he needed throughout the night.

Eventually, I got used to boiling countless bottles and nipples, changing disgusting diapers and soothing seemingly unstoppable cries. I guess it was not too hard for me because I was the oldest of the five children in my mom's house, and there had always been a baby crying or needing some kind of attention. The youngest two were boys so my practice with them had paid off. Although I was exhausted and felt entirely too young for the job, I felt that I was handling being a single mother to my own baby boy pretty well so far.

However, looking down at my stomach, I was concerned about having to live with the changes to my body forever. I had a big stomach, and for some reason it was much darker than the rest of my skin. I also had a long scar across my abdomen where my son had been removed from my body and stretch marks that looked like tiger scratches down my sides. I was only fifteen and thinking my body that already had so many issues was now even worse. But my stomach soon flattened out and eventually returned to its normal color. I still had the scar from the C-section; however, it was barely noticeable and nobody had any business seeing that area of my body anyway. I was upset about the stretch marks on my sides that matched the back of my legs because they were not going anywhere and everything I read said that stretch marks were permanent. Well, I was a mother and had all the evidence to prove it. However, I still needed to prove that God had answered my prayers and made Markus my son's father.

Lessons Learned:

- ♥ **Spend money wisely.** The limited money I had was not wasted on anything I didn't absolutely need. I constantly evaluated how I spent the little money I had and looked for ways to do better at saving it to provide for my son and his future.

- ♥ **Take pride in little things and appreciate everything.** I began to live my life by the belief that if I was faithful over a few things, God would bless me with more. I was so thankful for the new-to-me bed I had been given and God eventually blessed me with the ability to buy any bed I wanted.

- ♥ **Don't give up.** For some people, going to school is hard enough. Juggling the responsibilities of motherhood with school assignments can seem impossible. No matter how hard it gets, stay in school and continue to push. I knew that working hard and getting an education meant that I wouldn't have to work as hard later in life.

- ♥ **Evaluate all resources.** God places people in our lives for a reason. The support of my resources of family and friends and the internal resource of my own creativity and determination was a key aspect of my entire life and the main reasons I was able to keep pressing forward.

Just Face It

So be strong and courageous! Do not be afraid and do not panic before them. For the Lord your God will personally go ahead of you. He will neither fail you nor abandon you.
-Deuteronomy 31:6

By the spring, my baby was old enough for us to take a blood test to find out for sure what I felt in my gut to be true yet I prayed was not. We would finally know whom Jaylan's father was-the guy who had violated me on my birthday a year ago or my ex-boyfriend, Markus.

Throughout my pregnancy and during the weeks after he was born, we acted like Jaylan was Markus' son. Well, Markus was hesitant to fully embrace my baby, but his mother certainly was not. Just like when I was pregnant, my baby and I spent a lot of time at her house and now that he was on the outside, she pointed directly to him and told her friends, "That beautiful boy is my grandbaby." However, we all knew it was possible that he was not.

On the day that we went to take the blood test, Markus and Kaye met my mother, Jaylan and me at a clinic in Jackson. Sitting in the waiting room in a seat directly across from Markus, I observed a scared little boy. Looking back at me, I'm sure he saw a scared little girl. As we sat with our mothers who chatted about everything but the reason why we were at the clinic, the nurse entered the waiting area.

First extending her hand towards Markus and then towards me, she said, "First, I'll take you back. We'll take a sample of your blood, and then we'll bring you and the baby back, mother."

She gave us a fake smile that said, *It is so sad to have these children here. This little girl doesn't even know who the father of her baby is.* As I had felt so many times before, I was embarrassed. I asked, *God, why do I have to keep facing people with my mistake? Everyone is judging me, and it's just not fair.*

When Markus returned to the cold, quiet waiting room, he looked straight ahead at his mother avoiding eye contact with me. Almost as if he knew what was happening, Jaylan started to squirm as he and I headed back to have our blood taken. Although I didn't like needles and didn't want my baby to get stuck, I was anxious to take the test and confirm that Markus was the father. As I strolled down the hall, I prayed. If Markus was his father, then my baby would have a daddy and another grandmother to love him and to help me raise him. If he was not the father, then my son would not have a father, and I would have to teach my baby boy how to be a man.

"Okay, mom, hold his finger real still," the nurse instructed me as she poked my baby's finger.

After finally finding a vein in my arm, she retrieved my blood too. Returning to the waiting room, I stared at my mother who wore the same face of disbelief I had seen when she confronted me about the pregnancy and as I was giving birth.

"Well, I guess we're about to finally find out," I exhaled glancing at Markus and his mother as I sat down in the chair next to my mother.

I was just ignorant of so many things and thought that we would get the results before we left the clinic. Instead, the nurse re-entered the waiting room and said, "Well, we're all done here. You should receive the results in the mail in about six weeks."

My internal scream shook my body, *Six weeks! You mean I have to wait another six weeks to find out who is the father of my baby?*

Back at my grandmother's house, I headed straight to my bedroom and placed my baby, who had fallen asleep, on the bed next to me. I stared at the yellowing ceiling as I replayed the events of the day in mind. Tears rolled down my face and into my hair as my heart continued to grow heavy. I still did not know who the father of my son was. *Lord, I thought this was the day that I would be put out of my misery and Markus and I could prepare to raise our son together. Why does this have to be so hard?* From the day my son was born, I had counted down to the date when I would know. However, I just had to wait even longer. During my not-so-patient wait, I found things to do to occupy my time.

Leaving my baby at home with my sweet grandmother each day, I returned to school and began my mad dash to catch up with my classmates. Homeschooling had taught me nothing, and I was fully six weeks behind everyone. I met with each of my teachers and developed plans for me to make up the class work and tests I had missed. Staying after school most days taking tests from the previous grading period, I then went home and studied for tests in the same subject for the current grading period that I would be taking the next day. Even though this was challenging and confusing, I did what I had to do to catch up. I refused to fall behind any further. By the time I accomplished that feat, I felt like I could do anything.

Before I returned to school, I had started going back to church. The confidence I gained after catching up at school made me feel better about facing the church members. Just as I had done whenever I went anywhere from the grocery store to the doctor's office with my baby, I balled up my fist and placed my baby in his carrier on the capitol letter L my right arm had become and his diaper bag and my purse on my left arm and headed into church. When I was finally able to sit down the bag of bricks I had carefully transported inside, my blood-red arm looked like it was only seconds away from falling off.

At first I was embarrassed walking into the church just as I had been when my stomach started growing, and everyone looked at me like I was another fast little girl whose behavior was exposed by a pregnancy. However, as I began to accept myself as a teenage mother, others accepted me too. I felt more comfortable at church and wanted to show off my beautiful baby rather than hide the fact that I had one. I was fifteen, and I was a mother. What they did not know, and neither did I, was who the father of my baby was.

Every day I anxiously checked the mail and finally the results arrived. Sorting through all the junk mail, I ran into the house and placed everything except my envelope on the kitchen table. I lowered myself onto the couch in the living room to read the letter. I took a long, deep breath and then opened it. It stated that with 99.7% certainty, Markus was *not* my son's father.

After the shock wore off, the tears broke the dam and flooded my face. Closing my drenched eyes, I saw my future. I was all alone raising a sad son, and I did not know what I was doing. Then a vision of how I had pictured our future with Markus appeared. Markus was throwing a ball our toddler.

But, no, Markus was not his father. The guy I knew only as Poppey was the father of my beautiful baby boy. I didn't even know where this Poppey character was or anything about him. I really didn't even want to know, but I had heard that he was a drug dealer in California. No, he had nothing to add to my son's life. Plus, I never wanted to see him again. I was sad and scared and left motionless.

When I could move again, I called Kaye and Markus to see if they had gotten their letter. Kaye answered the phone, and I stuttered over the tears that were forming again, "Um, hey Kaye. This is Summer. Did you..."

She interrupted, "Yeah, baby. We got it. You know he's still my grandbaby though."

That gave me some comfort, but deep down I knew that since the baby was not Markus's I was not going to have their help with him no matter what her initial intentions might have been.

After a moment of silence, I asked, "Is Markus there?"

"Naw, he's up town with his friends, but he knows, baby."

"Ah...um...okay. I guess I'll call him later."

"Okay, baby."

She sounded a little disappointed, but I sensed that she might have been relieved.

When I finally talked to Markus, I found out that he was relieved too. Waiting nervously for him to answer the phone, I called back.

"Hello," stated a calm voice on the other end.

Not nearly as composed, I responded with a bit of an attitude, "Well, you're not a daddy."

"Yeah, I know. Summer, I can't lie and say that I'm upset. I'm not ready for a baby."

The frog in my throat and the sting in my heart would only let me say, "O...kay," as the phone slowly slid down the side of my face finally landing in my lap. I didn't expect him to be so happy when I was so hurt. Looking down at the phone, I could hear "Summer, Summer..." but I couldn't even pick the phone back up. He was relieved, and I was distraught. I needed *him* to be the daddy.

Lessons Learned:

♥ **Disappointments will come, but they don't dictate the end of the story.** Outcomes will not always be as we expect them or want them, but God has a plan for our lives and will work everything out if we do our part and trust him.

♥ **Helping myself made others want to help me.** Before asking for help, I did whatever I could for myself. I applied this practice throughout my life, and I believe people help those who first help themselves. Even when people wouldn't help me, I never used that as an excuse to not do what I needed to do to improve our lives.

Get to Work

"Lazy people want much but get little, but those who work hard will prosper." -Proverbs 13:4

Once I finally got caught up on my school work and no longer had the stress of wondering who my baby's father was, I could relax a little. Well, I don't know if relax is the best word, but I was able to resume my extracurricular activities at school and try to feel and act like the pre-baby me. I felt good about getting back to some of my normal activities, but then I realized that I was a mother and need to provide for my son. Because I was so young and had no income up to that point other than the little child support my dad paid my mother each month, I had been on government assistance receiving WIC for the beginning of my son's life. It was then that I decided that I wanted to contribute more to my household. Providing milk, cereal and juice wasn't nearly enough. I had to do more. Seeing the lives of other women I knew who received government assistance, I decided that life wasn't for me. I wanted to one day be able to have anything and go anywhere I wanted rather than waiting on food stamps or a check to pay my bills. I never wanted to be dependent on anyone let alone the government, and I had to start making my own money.

My friend Cynthia had been working at a local fast food restaurant for the past few months so I asked her to recommend me to the manager. When my son was almost a year old, I filled out the application and was hired on the spot, received my shirt and cap, and started working two days later. Working nearly every day of the week, I could not rely on my friends to take me to work like they had done for school. Catching a ride to school was no problem because they were going to the same place, and riding home was the same because one of my friends lived down the street from my grandmother. However, going to work was a different story. My grandmother couldn't drive and did not own a vehicle, and my mother would be at work in Bolivar when I needed to get work.

I needed my own transportation. I asked my dad to help me buy a car, and he said he would, but when was the question. I needed a car right away because I had already become a pest bumming rides my first week on the job. My dad didn't understand the urgency of my request, and like in other situations, I took matters into my own hands. I have never been the most patient person, and I always believed that if someone wants something to happen then they can't wait on other people to do it for them.

Loading Jaylan's car seat into my mom's minivan, we drove to Memphis where she figured I could get a better deal on a car. We spent the entire day looking at cars, and I test drove a few. I finally settled on a white Dodge Neon and decided to go with the four-door model so that I could easily get to Jaylan in his car seat that would be positioned in the back seat of the car.

The car was brand new and fit me perfectly. I would be paying my own car note with only the money I earned from my job so I had to keep the note very low. After I signed the paperwork, I was the proud owner of my very first car. Tired from the long day, my mother and I prepared to head back to Jackson that night. I took Jaylan's car seat out of my mother's van and put it in its new, permanent spot in the back seat of my new car, and we trailed my mother back to Jackson.

I needed a car because I had a job, and I needed a job because I had a baby. I usually worked about fifteen hours each week and was typically on the schedule starting at 5:00 or 6:00 PM so my routine was to come home from school around 3:00 PM on days when I did not have any afterschool meetings or activities.

Once I got home from school, I relieved my grandmother of her babysitting duties and brought my baby to my bedroom or the living room and placed him in his swing, walker, playpen or carrier and started on my homework. I just wanted to have him in my presence if only for a short period of time. With only about an hour on some days to do my homework before leaving for work, I changed into my uniform and headed to work. Although I was sad about leaving my baby and putting so much work on my grandmother, I was proud to be making my own money and of my ability to contribute to the household. I felt mature and responsible and like I was finally holding my own. Taking orders, cooking fries, wiping tables, and cleaning bathrooms brought the close of my shift quickly. I finished work through the week around 10:45 PM and later on the weekends and then headed home to my other job.

Driving home from work in my little white Neon, I played what was still my favorite cassette, "I Will Survive" constantly fighting to stay encouraged through my situation and also to help me stay awake after the long days at school and work. As I jiggled my keys to unlock the front door of the house after work each night, I could hear my toddler's quick steps as he ran from my grandmother's bedroom in the back of the house to greet me. I looked down at my child and passed the big cup of pink lemonade I always brought home from work into the little arms reaching towards it, "Cup, cup, Mommy."

His vocabulary had grown from his first word "ball" and the second, but most important word he'd ever say, "Mommy". At first it was just me getting a cold drink at the end of my shift, but it soon was all about Jaylan and the satisfaction of seeing him want something that I could provide him.

Once he calmed down, I began my attempt to put him to sleep so that I could finish my homework that I usually never was able to finish before going to work. I was in honors classes that required more work and more reading so I stayed up late getting it all done. I pleaded with God, *Please help me. I'm tired of doing this. I love my baby, but I just want to be a normal teenager.*

The next morning, I woke up early for school that started at 7:00 AM. I disposed of the diapers I had thrown beside my bed the night before and washed the empty bottles that rested in my headboard before getting dressed and heading out the door. Each day the process got a little less difficult, but it was never easy.

Later that year, I added a second job. My aunt worked at a coffee shop and asked me to help out one day because they needed a hostess to greet customers so that they would not leave when they saw the restaurant was full. Although I was still shy, the job was pretty easy and helped me overcome my shyness and earn money at the same time. From 7:00 AM-2:00 PM on Saturday's, I worked at the coffee shop and went to my other job from 5:00 PM until the restaurant closed.

I worked both of these jobs for nearly two years and earned money to help support my child. Although I was often tired and spent time away from my son, I really enjoyed my time at work and learned several valuable lessons at both jobs that would help me throughout my lifetime.

Lessons Learned:

- ♥ **Don't let children be an excuse.** Yes, I had a baby, but rather than allowing that to be the reason for me not to go to school or get a job, it was the main reason why I had to get busy.

- ♥ **Don't wait on other people to figure it out.** I was the mother, and I wanted a good life for me and my baby. I had to make a way for myself. As much as some people loved me, they couldn't live my life for me.

- ♥ **Working builds self-esteem.** Having a job made me feel important. The work that I did on my job mattered, and having a job gave me the resources to help my baby and my grandmother. Having a job and earning money taught me time and money management skills, the importance of a good attitude, and the value of hard work and a good work ethic.

- ♥ **Keep showing appreciation for help.** Going to school and working a job would not have been possible for me without the help of my grandmother who kept my son for me while I continued my education and earned an income to help support our family.

The End and the Beginning

No, despite all these things, overwhelming victory is ours through Christ, who loved us. -Romans 8:37

I was in the 10th grade when I had my baby, started my first job, bought my first car and somehow remained involved in school activities. The two years after giving birth proved to be challenging at best, but I made the most of them and tried to be as normal as possible while still taking care of my responsibilities as a mother. One of the greatest blessings to my life and my situation was my grandmother. Because of her help, I was able to go to school and still participate in school activities even if that meant after school meetings. I was able to work not one, but two, jobs. And I was able to do this with the comfort of knowing that my son was being taken care of by the best person in the world I could imagine him being with.

My family supported me because they saw my commitment and my effort to being a good mother. Commitment and effort were very much needed in every aspect of my life especially with raising Jaylan. Besides the expected daily challenges of feeding, changing and soothing a crying baby and a couple of episodes of him sitting in his car seat kicking the back of my seat while I drove, my first major challenge with my son was potty training.

Because pampers and eventually pull-ups were such a burden on my limited budget, I began my efforts to potty train as soon as he tried to walk. Using a hand-me-down potty from my six-year-old brother, I confronted the task. In the beginning, his potty had a permanent position in the living room in front of the couch. Although it wasn't very pleasant to see, Jaylan's potty was his seat. While I sat on the couch, he sat on the potty. Jaylan watched television, ate food, and played with his toys all while he sat on his potty. Whatever he was doing, his bottom was glued to it until something came out. It didn't take long for him to catch on to the concept of using the potty because he did not want to stay on it any longer than he needed.

The next step in potty training was even harder. Unfortunately for our training efforts, I did not have all the same body parts as my little man. Neither did my grandmother. He needed someone with the same anatomy as him to show him how to use the bathroom standing up. I did the best I could by holding his hand and showing him how to hold his pee tool, but I also relied on my brothers to show him what to do whenever they were around which wasn't often enough. After several occurrences of spraying the entire toilet and several walls, he caught on. Potty training didn't relieve me of the job of cleaning nasty toilets and pee-soaked walls, but conquering the challenge made me feel like I could accomplish anything.

When Senior Superlatives time came around and our class submitted nominations for various categories, many of my friends were chosen. So was I. During our time in high school, we had made the most of it by joining clubs, attending school functions and games, and just having fun all while maintaining good grades. Although I had a little life at home to take care of, my education was very important to me. I knew that bettering myself was the only way I would be able to truly take care of my child on my own one day. Because I had given birth two years earlier and returned to school with even more fervor than when I left, my classmates chose me as Most Likely to Succeed.

I had only one other competitor. She was a cute, popular cheerleader who I figured would win. When she didn't, she blurted into a crowd, "Our Miss Most Likely to Succeed has already succeeded...she has a baby!"

Yes, I won. My classmates realized then that being successful did not mean being perfect, not having setbacks or making no mistakes. Instead, it was determined by how the person handled those setbacks and overcame obstacles.

By the end of my senior year, I felt even better about myself and my status as a teenage mother. As a little girl, I was skinny and ugly with bucked teeth and sparse hair. In middle school, I had wide hips and stretch marks. In high school, I had acne, the memory of rape and the embarrassment of walking around pregnant and then the stigma of being a teenage mother. Even with all of that, I was finally okay being me.

When my guidance counselor was asked to choose a student to be featured on the local news station's "Senior Salute" program, she chose me. I was honored to have been selected, especially since I was a teenage mother. One senior from each of the other five high schools in Jackson was chosen with commercials airing for each of them, but every time I looked up I saw my commercial. "It's on! It's on! I'm on TV. I'm on TV!" I yelled to my grandmother as I dialed my mother's number to tell her to turn to the channel to see me.

Running during the same time period was another commercial I had been asked to do. Although I was unable to participate in a fashion show my friends did for a clothing store in the mall called 5-7-9, which were the sizes of the clothes in the store, because my wide hips pushed me to wearing a size eleven, I was asked to be a model for a local prom store. Flattered to have even been asked, I accepted but immediately worried about finding a dress to fit my disproportionate body. I tried on dozens of dresses and finally found a sparkly navy blue one that looked halfway decent on me, and the store owners produced the commercial with me and a few other young ladies standing almost like mannequins as we smiled and displayed the dresses. The prom store commercial seemed to run in even heavier rotation than the other commercial.

"Grandma! I'm on again!" I exclaimed and pointed to the TV at least the first five times I saw each commercial.

I couldn't believe this nappy headed, buck-toothed girl with acne and stretch marks and even a baby was on TV in not one, but two commercials. I did not get paid money for the commercials, but I did get paid with increased self-confidence that money could not buy. I was pretty enough to be asked to be in their commercial, and my body issues did not stop them from choosing me, and neither did the fact that I was a mother. I thought, *Maybe I'm not so bad after all.*

Although I modeled a prom dress for a commercial, I didn't even plan to attend my own prom because I did not have a date. After a few unsuccessful attempts at finding a date, I asked one of the most fun people I knew, my sister Brandy who was a sophomore. Because we could not afford to buy prom dresses, my mother made two beautiful dresses for us. Mine was a metallic lavender material made from three different dress patterns, a size six for my bust, a four for my waist, and a twelve for my hips. Jaylan sat on the floor watching and probably wondering what I was doing as I cut out my own pattern and material to help my mother. Brandy's dress was plum and just one size pattern as her body was more proportioned than mine. Dawning our new dresses, clear Cinderella slippers, makeup and fancy pinned up hair do's, we were ready to go. I felt beautiful in spite of my insecurities. Because I had worked so hard getting through school and on my jobs, my mother gladly volunteered to be my babysitter for the night. Brandy and I headed to the prom in my freshly washed white Neon.

Enjoying myself with my sister and my friends at the prom, I reflected on how things were really looking up for me and I knew it was because I worked for it. I worked hard and then God worked harder. Many times I felt like I was fighting a losing battle. Sometimes, I thought about giving up. I was working so hard and moving so fast, and I just wanted to rest. Most days, I cried and felt sorry for myself because no one understood what I was going through or how I felt. No one could help me on the inside, and sometimes no one could help on the outside either. However, I decided I wanted a good life for my son and that he was indeed my son and not my brother. I wanted the best for him and for me, and I made the decision to do what it took to make that happen.

I quickly learned that sometimes I just had to encourage myself when no one else would or even knew I needed encouragement. Although I knew people cared for me and wanted to see me succeed, no one ever said, "Summer, now you need to finish high school and strive to be at the top of your class." No one said, "Get involved in other activities to broaden your horizon, help you figure out what you want to do in your life and get the most out of your educational experience." No one pushed me.

I was the only one who knew how hard it was for me to look at my baby every morning knowing he did not have a father then go to school and do what I had to do there knowing that everyone from teachers to students knew that I had a baby and were constantly judging me no matter what I did. I was the one who rushed home from school or after school meetings to catch a few minutes with my son while I quickly started my homework that I would not finish until after a five or six hour shift at work. With God's help and my grandmother babysitting my son while I was at school and work, I did it. Yes, I still felt bad being away from him and relying on my grandmother's help so much, but I saw the big picture. I knew the sacrifice then would position me to take care of him all by myself later, and I would be able to take care of my grandmother too.

My hard work in the classroom had paid off, and I graduated in the top ten of my class. Jaylan's mother was number eight of nearly three hundred of her classmates. Being in the top ten was not my goal. I just wanted to do my best. Although I would love to think I was extremely smart, the truth was that I was more of an average student. The difference was that I worked harder. Maybe it was in me all along, but I felt like having someone else depending on me pushed me even harder. I was determined not to let having a baby deter my dreams of being successful, and I had taken a huge step in that direction. I was ready for the next step.

Three years to the day after the incident that resulted in my pregnancy, I participated in an awards day program with my graduating class. In spite of the happy occasion, it was the anniversary of the rape and it was also my eighteenth birthday. Throughout the day, I relived the sadness and confusion of that night and the years that followed and wondered, *How different would my life be if I had never entered that room or if I had left when he came in or if I had screamed when he touched me?*

As we sat lined up on the arena floor, our guidance counselor went down her list alphabetically calling out the names of the students who had received scholarships and announced where they would be attending college. When she called each name, the student stood up and was recognized.

Although I'm sure everyone was anxious to be acknowledged, I was particularly proud because I wanted to show people I had done it. Not only was the teen mother of the class graduating, but I had also earned a full scholarship. When they found out I was pregnant, many people had counted me out and gave up on their expectations for my future. That day I was hurt with the reminder of what had happened to me, but I looked forward to the proud moment that was about to happen and, in some small way, replace that memory. I pictured myself, mother of two-year-old Jaylan, standing before my classmates and the crowd while the counselor announced, "With a 3.89 grade point average, Summer Owens will be attending the University of Memphis on the Emerging Leaders scholarship." Applause would follow as I basked in my moment of glory.

I never got that chance. The student's name to my right was called, and his scholarship announced. The student to my left didn't receive one, but the boy to his left was then called with his scholarship announced. I panicked and wondered, *What about me? How could she skip me? Okay, surely she will realize her mistake, come back to my name, and give me the chance to stand up before the crowd.* I sat there during the program and figured everyone in the audience and even my classmates who did not know I had gotten a scholarship looked at me thinking, "I knew she couldn't do it."

The program ended, and we were dismissed. I was hurt. I did not get my "See! Proved you wrong!" moment. My mother hugged me after the ceremony because she knew I was disappointed, but I don't know if she even realized the deeper reason why I was so sad that day. Spotting the guidance counselor on the crosswalk, I held back tears and inquired, "Was my name not on the list?"

"What do you mean, dear?"

"I received a scholarship, but it didn't get called out today. What happened?"

"I'm not sure," then she patted me on the back smiling and said, "The important thing is that you got one."

I walked away thinking, *Then why do we even have Awards Day? Happy Birthday to me...*

Yes, I was hurt, but I did realize that the most important part was that I would be going to college even when my parents could not afford it. Not only had I received a full scholarship for good grades and campus and community involvement that paid my tuition and room and board, but I also received financial aid. Thanking God for the scholarship and the financial aid He had blessed me with, I realized the acknowledgment was not nearly as important as the fact that I now had the finances to attend college when my parents had never saved a dime to send me and now would never have to.

The day after the awards program was the culmination of my high school career - my graduation. Marching in like a sea of algae, over 300 green caps and gowns filled the arena floor. I waited impatiently for my turn to receive my diploma and move my gold tassel to the right of my cap. I applauded in my seat as my friends crossed the stage before me. It was almost my turn.

Finally, my row was instructed to stand. I took a deep breath, stood up and strutted to the stage with my row. My gold tassel dangled from my cap and my gold honor cord hung from my neck as I approached the stage. "Sum-mer Cur-teece O-wens" was enunciated nice and slowly, and I nervously but proudly strolled across the stage shaking hands with my principal and stopping for a picture once I made it to the end of the stage. It was official. I could check completing high school off my list.

After the ceremony, all the graduates headed outside to find their families. I finally found mine on the crowded crosswalk filled with new graduates and their loved ones. It was the same crosswalk I had traveled the past four years to get from class to class. The same crosswalk where a big, pregnant Summer fell on her knees after someone stepped on the untied shoelace of her sneakers.

My mother placed the then two-year old Jaylan in my outstretched arms as he reached for the graduation cap I had tossed into the air and retrieved. Placing the cap on his head, I hugged him tightly and proudly exclaimed, "We did it!"

This was a commencement ceremony; not an ending ceremony. And it truly was just another beginning for me.

Lessons Learned:

❤ **Don't do it for other people or acknowledgments.** The recognition may never come. Do it for yourself. Do it for your child.

❤ **Find a way. Make a way.** I knew going to college was my ticket to a better life for me and my son, but my parents did not have the money to pay for my college education. I, not my mother or anyone else, sought and applied for several scholarships. I did the research and filled out the paperwork to apply for financial aid. My diligence paid off, and I ended up going to college for free.

❤ **Make a decision to succeed, and stop making excuses.** I could have easily decided that it was too hard to attend school and to be a mother and given up, but I knew that giving up then would mean giving up on my future and my son.

❤ **I can do anything I set my mind to.** Potty training a little boy was hard for me as woman. I did not have the same anatomy as him, but I showed him how to use what he had to do what he needed to do. I took that lesson and applied it to my own life. I did not have what everyone else had, and I *did* have something a lot of others did not- a baby. I learned how to do what I needed to do with what I had.

Preparation for a New Beginning

This means that anyone who belongs to Christ has become a new person. The old life is gone; a new life has begun!
-2 Corinthians 5:17

My grandmother agreed to keep Jaylan for me while I started college to allow me time to get acclimated to my new environment. However, I still did not take my responsibility of being a mother lightly. Even if I was away at school, I needed to be close enough to visit my son often and still contribute as much as I could to raising him. I only applied to schools within three hours of Jackson where my son would be. I chose the University of Memphis which was only an hour away but still far enough for me to feel like I had truly left home. In smaller cities and towns, many of the people who stay in those towns when they graduate from high school halt their progression and their minds stop growing. They do not experience anything new and cannot envision change or improvement for their lives because they do not know anything other than what they have been exposed to their entire lives. I wanted to experience something bigger than what I already knew.

Because of my grade point average, college entrance exam scores, volunteer work and extracurricular involvement, I received the Emerging Leaders Scholarship. In applying for this scholarship, I had to develop a portfolio demonstrating my leadership abilities. My school activities were a central part of the presentation, but I also had something very special that not many other candidates had.

I had very meaningful volunteer experience, awards and acknowledgements for my volunteer work, and most importantly, a wonderful, heartfelt letter of recommendation from the volunteer coordinator, Susanne. In the letter, she spoke of me as a volunteen, but she also spoke of me as a person whom she had seen overcome tremendous obstacles and still remained positive and committed to being successful. While I was shredding and filing papers at the mental hospital, I had no idea I was setting myself up to earn a full scholarship. Receiving that scholarship was my payday for the long hours during those hot summers and for my hard work in the classroom and outside.

I had received graduation gifts of luggage, gift cards, and money, and with the cash and gift cards, my mother, Jaylan and I headed to Wal-mart. With my baby sitting in the front of the basket, I pushed the cart through the aisles loading it with items I needed for my dorm room. It was the most exciting time of my life. Yet, the feeling was bittersweet. I thought, *Am I wrong to be so excited when I'm about to leave my baby? Isn't it a good thing that I'm going to college? Well, why do I feel guilty one minute and excited the next?*

As a young woman, I was starting a new chapter in my life. However, I would be starting it without my son. Beyond grateful that my grandmother agreed to keep my baby while I went to college, I also felt guilty for leaving her with *my* responsibility. Deep down I knew that getting a good start in college was what I needed to ensure I would not spend my life depending on her or anyone else to take care of my son or me. Focusing on the big picture, I tried to maintain my excitement about my new adventure.

Preparing for college I attended Frosh Camp and New Student Orientation before starting school. Led by upperclassmen, Frosh Camp was completely about preparing freshmen for college life. Each day of the week-long camp was full of activities designed to help us get to know each other and learn more about the campus and college life. At orientation, I was paired with an academic advisor who helped me assess my interests and plan a schedule based on the fact that I was still unsure of what my major would be. Orientation guides gave us a tour and told us about life on campus.

I was excited and thankful that my friends, Bilicia and Chinitra, were going to school with me, but I had not been able to talk them into attending Frosh Camp and orientation with me. Before the events, I considered backing out because I didn't know anyone else going. However, it was then that I realized that I could not wait on my friends to do things with me in college or in life. I had to make things happen for myself whether anyone else joined me or not.

I missed Jaylan while I was away, but Frosh Camp and orientation were the best activities I could have participated in to help ensure my success in college. I enjoyed them both so much that I applied and was accepted to become a camp counselor and an orientation guide the following summer.

Returning to my grandmother's house after orientation, I grabbed my toddler and squeezed him tightly. I thought, *I don't want to leave my baby, but this school feels so right. Surely, I'm doing the right thing for both of us. I can't believe I'll be leaving you soon, baby.*

All the items going with me to my new dorm room including my computer, a hunter green trunk where I would eventually store my Ramen noodle supply and other snacks, a tall clothes hamper full of towels, and a laundry basket with detergent and cleaning supplies sat in a corner of my grandmother's small living room waiting to be loaded in the cars when it was finally time to move to Memphis. When it was time to go, my mom and dad each arrived at my grandmother's house. We loaded up my little Neon and my dad's truck and headed to Memphis. I was beginning my new journey temporarily away from the child I was about to kiss goodbye. Looking at his confused face and holding back my tears, I explained, "Mama is about to go away to school for a little while, but I'll be back in a little bit. You're going to stay with GG. I'm going to call you, okay? Love you!"

GG was the cute name my grandmother had established for her great grandchildren to call her, and he understood what staying with GG meant, but he had no idea I was going on an extended school visit. Only I felt the torture of the departure but I tried to let my excitement about college overshadow it.

Slowly waving his tiny hand he uttered, "Bye, Mommy."

The tears pushed through and quietly rolled down by cheeks as I kneeled and wrapped my arms around him. I thought, *Bye, Mommy. Am I really about to leave my baby? What is he thinking? Does he think I don't love him? Will he stop loving me? Does he think I won't come back? Does he even care? Will he start calling my grandmother, "Mama"? Will I be replaced? Will I ever be able to truly come back for my son? Am I doing the right thing?*

Lessons Learned:

♥ **Don't wait on friends or anyone else to do what needs to be done.** Decide what's best and just do it even if you have to do it alone.

♥ **Sacrifice.** Sometimes sacrifice is necessary to reach the ultimate goal.

♥ **If it's too easy, it's probably not worthwhile.** I was doing the hardest things in my life so it had to have a huge impact.

It's a Different World

Don't copy the behavior and customs of this world, but let God transform you into a new person by changing the way you think. Then you will learn to know God's will for you, which is good and pleasing and perfect. -Romans 12:2

As we headed to Memphis, my thoughts flip-flopped between my son's sad goodbye and my life on campus, but I tried to focus on school and our future. I couldn't wait to see the room Chinitra and I would share, and I was anxious to meet our suite mates. I wondered, *Will they be like Chinitra and me? Will they be fun? I hope they are clean.* Then I began to worry about the campus and my classes. *How will I find all of my classes? I hope I don't get lost. Will I fit in? Will the work be too hard?* All of these questions began to crowd my head and my excitement turned into anxiety before we made it to Memphis.

Luckily, we made it to campus before my anxiety overwhelmed me. Pulling into the parking lot of my dorm, we saw hundreds of other students were moving in too. We first unloaded the big items on the back of my dad's truck and headed inside. I had gotten my room assignment earlier and knew that my room was on the 7th floor. When we got inside the building, we waited in the tiny hallway with the huge crowd for about ten minutes for an elevator. Finally, we determined that it would take us hours to get all my stuff moved in if we waited on that elevator. The only other option was to take the stairs; reluctantly, we began our climb.

Like many other students and their parents, we began our ascent up seven flights of stairs carrying everything from clothes and comforters to a computer and a microwave. On one of our trips up to our room, we ran into our new suite mates, Melanie and Erania. Chinitra and I liked them right away and looked forward to talking to them more once we were done unloading vehicles. They actually were a lot like us. They had been friends since childhood and were very friendly and silly too. We knew right away that we would have a great year with them. Bilicia was a few floors down from us, but she might as well have been our third roommate because she was with us all the time anyway.

We finally got all moved in, our parents headed home, and we spent the rest of the night unpacking and organizing our small dorm room and getting to know our suite mates. We placed matching comforters on our beds, and I hung a picture of Jaylan and me that I had painted in high school above my bed. Walking through our adjoining bathroom, we knocked on the door to our suite mates' room to chat with them before retiring for the night. We talked until we couldn't keep our eyes open and planned to compare schedules and walk the campus the next day.

Chinitra and I then staggered back to our room, and then it hit me that I was not with my baby. I hadn't even talked to him since I left. I finally called and talked to him as best he could.

"Jaylan, hey it's mommy," I started.

"Mommy?"

"Yeah, baby. It's mommy. Whatcha doin'?"

"Nothing," he replied in baby talk.

"Okay, I'm about to go to sleep. I just wanted to tell you goodnight and I love you."

"'K. Nite-nite!"

Slowly hanging up the phone, I turned the light off above my bed and cried myself to sleep. I felt so sad and so guilty. All the excitement of the day had worn off and reality had set in that this was going to be a long, hard year for me.

Starting college was exciting for me and was an opportunity to meet a whole new set of people. I knew this would also mean new people to question my situation. In this new place, whenever someone found out I had a baby, I observed as their minds tried to calculate when I must have given birth. For the rest of my life, whenever I entered a new environment I experienced this. Yes, I was young, and yes I was a mother.

And I missed my baby. I spent the first semester going back and forth to Jackson on the weekends while trying to be a regular student. I was attending school on the Emerging Leaders

Scholarship which required me to be involved in different organizations on campus. Each year, my level of responsibility in the organizations increased. Just like in high school, I enjoyed being involved in activities outside of class work. Actually, my organizational involvement was what helped me to enjoy college the most and helped me cope with being away from Jaylan.

Every night I called him for what I considered a conversation. At the end of our exchange neither of us wanted to say goodbye. Going back and forth laughing we said, "You hang up."

"No, you hang up, mommy."

"You hang up, sweetie."

"No, you."

Finally, I would say, "Let's count to three and both of us hang up."

In unison we would say, "One, two, three," and sometimes we would both hang up the phone, but most of the time neither of us would. Instead, we would laugh again and say, "You were supposed to hang up."

Eventually, I started bringing my toddler back to Memphis with me for a week at a time. He secretly slept in my dorm room and kept my roommate and suitemates entertained. When I needed to spank him at night, I took him to my car so that he would not disturb the entire dorm.

"You're too hard on him, Summer," I was often told by friends and classmates.

"No, you don't understand. I'm raising a man by myself. One day, he'll be much bigger than me. He has to learn to respect me while he's little. Yeah, he's cute, but he still has to behave."

During his visits, I took him to class with me because I had no other choices. We sat near the door in case we needed to slip out for any reason-misbehavior, bathroom break, whatever. I sat him at a desk next to me and gave him paper and crayons and instructed him to practice writing his name, letters and numbers. I never had to leave class early because he was always able to sit quietly through an entire class.

Outside of class, I tried to entertain him. Never athletic at all, I did my best to do the things my little boy enjoyed doing. Most days after class, we went to the park. Tossing a yellow Nerf baseball was something I got really good at doing, and he was a pro at swinging the plastic, red bat. We enjoyed our time together, but I could only keep him in the dorm for a short period of time before my resident advisor would notice. Returning him back to Jackson always saddened me, but I did what I had to do.

The entire ride back to Jackson, I pictured my baby sitting on the bed in my dorm room, walking or being carried across campus, or sitting on Melanie's bean bag watching cartoons in my suite mate's room.

Returning from Jackson to my home in the dorm was always hard, but I knew in my heart that getting my degree was the best thing I could do for myself to be a good mother to Jaylan.

I continued to stay busy on campus, and in the second semester of my freshman year something else soon came up to occupy a lot of my time. Chinitra, Bilicia and I knew from the time we had visited Chinitra's sister for her Alpha Kappa Alpha probate show when we were in the eleventh grade that we wanted to be members of the sorority.

Our opportunity came during the second semester of our freshmen year. Although I had a 4.0 grade point average and was active on campus, I wondered how I would be viewed because I had a baby. Proud of my accomplishments but still ashamed to say I had a baby out of wedlock, I was always fearful of the judgment of others especially these ladies. After attending an interest meeting and going through the application process, the three of us found out we were selected. Yes, Summer, teenaged mother of Jaylan, was chosen to be an AKA woman.

We then met and bonded with our line sisters, the other ladies who were accepted with us. Many of these ladies ended up playing significant roles in my future accomplishments in several ways but primarily by helping me with my son.

I spent the next three years focused on AKA by developing programs and participating in a leadership capacity for our chapter. That semester was unbelievably busy, and I was unable to bring Jaylan to Memphis or visit him in Jackson as often. I did, however, manage to maintain my 4.0 grade point average and vowed to myself to make up the time I had lost with my son. I looked forward to the end of my freshman year and going home for the summer to be with him.

Finally, the end came and so did my nineteenth birthday. Rather than being happy, I spent most of the day crying to myself. Occasionally, someone would catch me or see that I was sad, but I did not talk about why. My baby was living, and I loved him. There was no need to constantly bring up the past. However, each birthday served as a reminder of my fifteenth birthday that changed my life forever.

That summer when Bilicia and I were heading home to Jackson, an accident occurred that made my plans for the summer even more challenging. Trailing Bilicia on the interstate with our cars full of the contents from our dorm rooms, I hit the trailer of an eighteen-wheeler while trying to get off of an exit behind Bilicia as she rushed off the road. My car was thrust to the side of the interstate just missing the stone barrier and on-coming traffic. Luckily, I was not hurt, but my car was nearly totaled and had to be towed back to Memphis. By the time Bilicia made it back, a tow truck had arrived to take away my car and all of its contents from my dorm room because none of it could fit in Bilicia's already packed car. I did not have my car for most of the summer, but I had my life and I was able to see my baby again.

Back home for the summer, I enrolled in a history class at the local community college to get a few credits out of the way while I was at home. I also got a job at a shoe store to pay for the course, to help out my grandmother, to pay my car note and to put aside money for the upcoming semester.

Although I was still paying a car note, I didn't have transportation to and from school and work. I had to rely primarily on my mother when she could let me borrow her van or transport me. Bilicia was a big help too, and it helped that she got a job at the shoe store too. I was back home with my son for the summer, but I was busy working and going to school just like

I had been doing since I could legally work so I really was not spending a lot of time with him. But I still knew it would all be worth it when I had a career and was able to support my child and have time to spend with him too.

It took a while, but I eventually got my car back with a little bit of the summer to spare. I had my independence back and no longer had to wait on someone else to take me where I needed or wanted to go. I finished up the summer working at the shoe store and completed the history class which I had hated attending all summer long. Although I made an A in the class, I decided summer school was not for me and I would just push myself to take more hours in the regular semesters. Like always, I was busy with work and school, but I still did the best I could at being a mother and focused on the day when I would be able to be a better mother.

Returning to campus that fall, I received a call from the INROADS office. During the last semester of my senior year of high school, representatives from INROADS, an organization developed to help minority youth transition into corporate America, visited our school and gave a presentation to a designated group of seniors. The students in that group were either in the top 10% of the graduating class, had scored over a 23 on the ACT college entrance exam or had a 3.5 or better GPA. As part of the program, INROADS students interviewed for internships and went through training for corporate America. However, in order to be part of the program, students had to be hired for the job they interviewed for. If chosen from the interview, the student would be an intern with that company each summer during his or her college career. That summer, my good friend Destiny and I interviewed for the same internship at a bank. Destiny got the internship, and I was very discouraged.

However, I was given another chance my sophomore year. Like always, God was showing me that he had my back and I was set up to interview for an internship in the marketing department of a major hotel corporation. I got the job and became the marketing intern for one of the hotel brands for my last three years of college.

As an intern, I learned a lot about marketing and working in corporate America that would prepare me for life and my future career more than I could have ever known at the time and more than I learned in the classroom. In some ways, I felt like I was back in my volunteer days doing small, unnoticeable tasks. However, I remembered how significant those tasks and my contributions were and realized I could make an even greater impact in my position as an intern. Taking what I learned as a volunteer, I applied an even greater work ethic to my new position and earned greater responsibility each year. The opportunity to coordinate the presence of the hotel chain in a national tradeshow which provided me with tremendous material to include in my portfolio that I later displayed and helped me secure future jobs was one of the major benefits.

Lessons Learned:

- ♥ **Get involved to help get connected to the school.** Joining campus organizations made me feel better about being in college and helped me to improve and learn more. The more involved I was, the more difficult it was to even consider quitting school.

- ♥ **Take nothing for granted.** I almost lost my life, but God kept me here for a reason. I am trying to fulfill my purpose.

- ♥ **Keep moving.** I thought the summer was time for a break, but when it came, I knew I didn't have time to sit around and relax. I had to keep going.

- ♥ **Take every opportunity to learn.** My internship provided me with tremendous experiences that led to other opportunities in my life. Like my volunteer experience, I had no idea it would lead to much more for me.

I've Got to Keep on Moving

So let's not get tired of doing what is good. At just the right time we will reap a harvest of blessing if we don't give up.
-Galatians 6:9

Sophomore year was even busier. Taking on moderate leadership roles, I became a committee chair for several organizations. With all of my on-campus responsibilities, I still took my responsibility as a mother very seriously. I resumed driving to Jackson most weekends and bringing Jaylan back to Memphis when I could. I was still taking him to class with me a lot, but I had two other options when I could not.

Between my friends and the Student Activities Council (SAC), I was covered. My friends, both old and new ones, helped me a lot. Sometimes my roommate and former suite mates watched him in their dorm rooms or even took him to class with them. And when joining SAC my freshman year, I never imagined I was positioning myself to have a babysitter. The director, Tammy, fell in love with my little man as soon as she met him. Since I was a committee chair, I had my own cubicle in the office as well as office hours to serve each week. Being in the office so much, I grew very close to Tammy and the other student leaders. In the office, Jaylan served my office hours with me and had fun playing with the toys and the big children who called themselves college students in the office. However, he was in the office with Tammy even when I was not. When Tammy had meetings, her secretary played babysitter until I got out of class to retrieve my child. Some nights, Tammy took Jaylan home with her to watch movies and play games. It was a welcomed break for me when I was bogged down with homework.

As for the other activities I was involved in, when we had meetings, Jaylan was right by my side in meetings and even at events. I did not plan any of it and probably couldn't have done it so well if I had tried to, but it worked out. God had it worked out for me. I had to keep doing my best. As much as I enjoyed having him there with me, I still had to take him back to Jackson the next weekend. However, I soon was not able to visit him whenever I wanted because I had to give up my car.

That semester the lease on my Neon was up, and I had to return my only means of transportation back to the dealership. I spent the remainder of the semester walking to class from the student apartments and riding to Jackson with my friends when they went home. Being dependent on them and their schedules, I had a hard time accepting that I couldn't see my baby whenever I wanted. On the flipside, I no longer had a car note. However, that couldn't last long so I began saving the little money I earned from my internship and any money left over from my scholarship and financial aid for a car.

That Christmas, Jaylan and I rode the bus to Nashville to visit my dad as I had done many times before. This time, I was planning to drive back in my new car. On the bus, little Jaylan sat on my lap, and his car seat was stowed under the bus with our luggage. During our visit to Nashville, my dad and I visited several car lots and by the time we were exhausted from looking, I decided on a green Pontiac Sunfire to match the pink and green AKA license plate I would proudly display on the front of my new car. That year a thick blanket of snow covered the ground as I drove slowly and carefully back to Jackson for a visit with my mother to show off my new car and to sadly drop Jaylan back off at my grandmother's house before I headed back to Memphis to start the second semester of my sophomore year.

Leaving him that time was particularly hard for me, and I'd had enough. I needed my son in Memphis with me permanently so I began to make preparations to make that happen. When I returned to Memphis, I began looking for an off-campus apartment. I needed a place of my own, but I had very little money.

I still wanted a place off-campus so that my son could live with me. To afford it, I needed a roommate. A roommate that could share bills that is. Jaylan would be third party living in the apartment, but it would be a while before he could contribute to the household. Just in time, the president of SAC let me know that she was looking for a roommate for an affordable apartment close to campus. I was still a member of several organizations on campus and a chairperson for SAC so I always had meetings on campus in addition to events and a class schedule that included both morning and evening classes. The apartment close to campus would allow me to go home between classes, meetings or events. Most importantly, my own apartment meant my son could officially live with me.

Once I was in my new apartment, I moved Jaylan to Memphis. It was not the nicest apartment in the world, but it worked for us. With two bedrooms, one bathroom that my roommate and I shared, a small living area and a tiny kitchen, we were proud of our first place off campus. Jaylan and I shared my small bedroom where the only furniture I had was the old bed I had treasured at my grandmother's house, a desk my mother had given me for Christmas one year and a dresser that I bought at a nearby thrift store for $20. Eventually, I saved enough money to buy an inexpensive pre-owned living room set and coffee tables and decorated as much as I could.

Although it had everything I absolutely needed, the apartment did not have a washing machine or dryer. Marching down the stairs from the second floor apartment, I lugged heavy laundry bags to a nearby laundromat. Jaylan and I spent quite a bit of time at that laundromat. Not having a minute in my day to spare, I made the most of that time. While the clothes washed, I did homework looking up at my toddler as he pushed the laundry cart or played with his action figures. The occasional barbershop visit was a similar experience except I didn't have to look up from my books to make sure he was okay. He sat safely in the barber chair while I relished having the time to myself to complete my work.

With Jaylan living with me, I was officially a full-time student, a part-time intern, and a full-time mother. Although I knew before I moved him to Memphis that my life would be challenging, I embraced my responsibility as his mother and figured out how to take care of him and manage everything I had going on at school including all my activities outside of the classroom. Making a friend who was also a student who lived in my apartment complex, I found some relief when Jaylan visited her and played games with her and her boyfriend while I did homework. She called him her little sidekick and even took him to basketball and football games with her whenever I couldn't. Thankful for all the help I had in Memphis, I was happy to be taking the pressure off of my grandmother and putting it where it belonged-on me.

Accepting my full-time responsibility also meant giving up my freedom. The year before, I enjoyed going out with my friends to parties or even just to dinner whenever I wanted. Adjustments had to be made when my baby joined me. I declined many invitations. "Summer, we're going to the party this weekend. Wanna go?" a friend would inquire.

"Um, if I can find someone to keep Jaylan," I stated knowing that I should invest in a tape recorder so that I could just press "play" every time I needed to give that response.

Usually, I couldn't find anyone to keep him because my babysitters were my friends, and my friends were the ones partying. When the question was, "Wanna grab something to eat?"

I occasionally responded, "Okay, but you know Jaylan has to go."

Sitting at a table full of girls, Jaylan spent just as much time with my friends as I did. However, conversations were always modified and eventually, the invitations out dwindled. My friends loved me and understood my situation, but I knew they got tired of hearing me say, "I have to find somewhere for Jaylan to go." Being a college student, partying and spending time with my friends was important. However, the top priority was school, and attending classes became a greater challenge with my new full-time job.

After a few consecutive days of taking Jaylan to class with me, I realized that I needed a better solution. Staying in the SAC office from time to time was fine when he was not in Memphis full-time, but I could not rely on Tammy to be a babysitter every day. Because my friends were full-time students like me, I couldn't bother them with keeping Jaylan regularly either. I had to come up with something. After a little bit of research, I was blessed with a wonderful alternative.

The university offered a daycare that provided childcare at a discounted rate to students. Each morning before I went to class, I dropped my four-year-old off at the daycare on the University of Memphis campus. Jaylan loved this daycare and so did I. The teachers loved Jaylan too. Exposed to adults most of the time from going to class with me and being with my friends, Jaylan needed and benefited from the interaction with children his age. Although he learned basics like the alphabet, counting, tying his shoes and writing his name from my grandmother and me, I welcomed the opportunity for him to start being taught in a more formal manner.

Attending the daycare until my senior year of college, Jaylan even had his own graduation ceremony that some of my friends attended. Even Dr. Carson, the Vice President of Student Affairs who had been instrumental in my decision to attend the University of Memphis, graced us with presence.

"Summer, you know, I really admire you and what you've been able to accomplish here at the university while still taking care of your son," Dr. Carson expressed as we waited for the program to start.

"Thank you. That means a lot to me, Dr. Carson," I shyly responded.

Sitting in the audience, I watched my baby walk across the stage to receive his first diploma. I stifled my tears as I observed the big smile on his little face as he stood in line with his very own classmates and stared out into the audience at me. I thought, *Lord, thank you. I survived my first year of being a student-mother by myself. Look at him up there. He's happy, he's learning and he's growing. And I'm still doing what I need and want to do for school. Plus, Dr. Carson even acknowledges my efforts. God, you are so good to me. This is just the beginning.*

During the graduation, I was thankful that I was able to ignore a burden I had been carrying for the few months prior to the ceremony. Earlier that year, my roommate informed me that she would be moving out of our apartment to live with one of her friends. Knowing that I couldn't make her stay and didn't want her to if she didn't want to be there, I said, "Well, okay. I guess I'll figure something out here."

Seemingly unconcerned with my dilemma, she moved out the next month taking the one television set we had in the whole apartment and leaving me to pay the half of the bills she once covered. I immediately panicked because I had no idea how I would manage paying the rent and all the bills by myself, plus food, my car note and Jaylan's daycare. I thanked God that my tuition and books were covered by financial aid and scholarship funds, but I just did not have the money to cover her half of all the bills too. With only the money from my part-time internship, my budget got even tighter. It still wasn't enough.

I wondered, *It's great that my schooling is paid for, but I have to have a place to live. I have to feed my child. What am I going to do? I don't have any friends who can be my roommate, and I can't let just anyone share a place with me and my son. How am I going to do this? Is now the time that I have to give up and move back home where I can live for free?*

One weekend my dad came to visit us. After a night of no television he surprised me with a trip to an electronics store where he purchased a 32 inch television set and a small TV stand for the apartment that had become just mine and Jaylan's. I didn't ask for it and hadn't even complained about not having a TV.

"Thank you so much. I really appreciate this. I can't believe you...," I tried to express my immense gratitude.

"That's what I'm here for," he replied as he began taking the stand out of the box for the three of us to begin assembly.

Always independent and trying to make a way for myself, I never expected a gesture like that from my dad. Before he left, he also gave me $300 to help with that month's bills. I accepted the money but vowed to get myself together so that I wouldn't need to use anyone else's money again. I just wanted to prove to my parents and especially to myself that I didn't need to be dependent on anyone.

To help with that promise, I kept my expenses as low as possible. When my roommate moved out and took the television, I canceled the cable. Even when my dad bought me a new TV, I never got the cable reconnected because I just could not afford it. For me, cable was an unnecessary expense so my son and I watched the few channels we could get and movies I borrowed from friends or Disney movies he had received as gifts from Susanne. I cut out all other "luxuries" and lived with only what we needed.

Looking for other forms of income, I applied for public assistance and attempted to secure child support. Many college students I knew received food stamps, and I knew that if I could get food stamps then I could use the money I spent on food to pay my bills. However, I was told that I did not qualify because I had a car in my name. Walking out of that office unsure of how I was going to make ends meet, I thought, *Why can people who don't work and won't try to make their lives better get help while I struggle to make things better for me and my son and can't get a dime? So many other students get food stamps and they only have to take care of themselves. I have a baby to feed. How is that right?*

When temporary government support was not an option, I turned to my last resort. Desperately needing any money I could get, yet not wanting to even think about what happened to me or the person who did, my mind teetered back and forth, *No, I can't do that. I need to just leave it alone. Why even bring him into the picture now? Do you know how bad that'll look? How can I face him? He probably doesn't even have a legal job. What money can he give me anyway? You never know, he might have some money. It's not fair for me to have to do this by myself. It's his fault I'm in this situation anyway. I have to at least try and see what I can get.*

"Can you help me find out, um, *his* real name?" I asked the sister of my cousin from California who had brought Poppey into my life that dreadful day.

"Yeah, I know it, but I think you need his social security number. I don't know how you can get that," she answered.

Armed with only his first and last name, I entered the child support office and completed the paperwork with as much information as possible. After a few months of no response from the child support office, I gave up on getting any help from the person who put me in my predicament. No welfare, no child support, no help. I concluded, *Alright, God, I guess you're telling me it's all on me.*

Although I was very upset with my roommate for leaving me in such a bind, my attitude towards her eventually improved and I embraced the fact that my son could then have his own bedroom. Although he didn't have a bed frame, he had a mattress and a box spring I got from my mom's house. Making another trip to the thrift store, I found a $20 dresser for him too. With a little of the money my dad had given me left over, I bought a gallon of sky blue paint. Painting the walls together, we laughed and ignored the fact that I was struggling. I also found an inexpensive reversible red/blue comforter and added colorful pillows with his favorite Disney characters to finish off his bed. Not only was my son with me in Memphis, but he had his own little space.

Lessons Learned:

- ♥ **Ask for and accept help when needed.** In order for me to have Jaylan at school with me, I sometimes needed someone to keep him for me. I asked and usually received the help I needed because I had proven that I was reliable and trustworthy and always showed my appreciation for the help. I never took anyone or their time for granted.

- ♥ **Faith without works is void.** God knows the outcome, but He charges us with the effort. From getting my scholarship and financial aid to child care, God showed me that I just had to work hard and stay focused on my goals and he would make a way for me.

- ♥ **I could make it without public assistance and child support.** When I felt desperate and needed money, my desire to receive public assistance or child support was not fulfilled. However, my son and I never missed a meal and always had everything we needed.

His Journey Begins

No eye has seen, no ear has heard, and no mind has imagined what God has prepared for those who love him.
-1 Corinthians 2:9

Jaylan celebrated his fifth birthday in our little apartment. At the rickety dining room table with painted green legs, my baby blew out the number five candle on his colorful cake. A handful of kids and more adults, my mother, grandmother and friends, participated in the momentous occasion. With my tiny budget, I created the best hot dogs, chips, cake and ice cream he had ever had. Five years had gone by fast, and this birthday was especially tough for me. Although he was still my baby, he was truly growing up and getting ready to start school.

Moving into a new apartment with Chinitra to share the bills, we prepared to start kindergarten. We went shopping for school supplies and even a couple of new outfits. I sat aside money from the previous paychecks to ensure I would have at least a few dollars to get my son off to a fresh start.

The night before his first day, I picked out a navy blue pair of shorts and a navy blue and white striped collared shirt which I ironed and placed over the chair in his bedroom. Placing the dark brown braided belt I found on sale on top of his freshly pressed clothes, I then pulled out his new dark brown sandals and put them on the floor beneath his clothes so that getting ready in the morning would be easy.

After I helped him take a bath before going to bed, he stepped up to the sink on the little, blue step stool I bought him to help him reach the sink to brush his teeth on his own. I stood in the doorway of the bathroom as he asserted his independence and remembered holding him up to the sink with my left arm and brushing his teeth with my right only a couple of months earlier. Demonstrating that he needed me less and less as he grew, I was torn on how to feel. *Shouldn't I be happy that he's growing up and can do more on his own?*

"Is it time to go to real school yet, mommy?" he excitedly inquired the next morning.

"Yes, baby. We're gonna go in a little bit," I explained as I pulled a sausage and biscuit out the microwave and poured him a glass of milk.

After getting dressed in the outfit we had carefully prepared the night before and throwing on his new back pack, we headed down the two flights of stairs of our apartment building to the little, green Sunfire.

"You excited about school, baby?" I asked halfway not believing he was starting kindergarten.

"Yes, ma'am," he responded turning his head towards me then looking back out the window.

"You know, you're a real big boy now!"

He laughed and asked, "For real?"

"Yep!"

Once at the school, I grabbed his hand and walked him into the cafeteria where we had been instructed to take the kindergartners. At the long table with little red, round seats that nearly touched the ground connected to it, I sat with my kindergartner and the rest of the parents and first time students until a teacher greeted the group. After a brief speech, the parents were politely dismissed. I thought, *But I didn't think we'd have to leave our babies on the first day. But he's just five years old. He needs me. There's no way he'll stay here with a bunch of strangers all day. He's not ready for that.*

I had a hard time leaving. I just could not believe it was real. The baby I had just brought home from the hospital was already in school. Eventually, I staggered out of the cafeteria, and, yes, a few tears were released.

"Bye, mommy!" he excitedly stated as he sat on the round seat with his backpack still attached. Waving and swinging his dangling legs, he continued, "See you in a little bit."

I thought, *What? You're supposed to be crying too! Aren't you scared? Don't you need me to stay here? I guess not.*

He sat at the long cafeteria table like a big boy and continued smiling and waving goodbye to me. He wasn't afraid at all.

For the rest of the week, I drove Jaylan to school passing all the children in the front of the apartment complex as they waited on the school bus. The second week, Jaylan asked, "Can I ride the bus like them?"

"Sure. That will be fun for you. You are such a big boy," I eagerly responded.

In the beginning, I drove him to the bus stop and waited with him until the bus came each morning. I eventually started walking him to the bus stop to get in a little exercise. Within a few weeks of the school year, a fourth-grade boy who lived in an apartment two stories below us saw Jaylan and me walking past his apartment as he headed to the bus stop by himself. In his sweet little voice and looking more at the ground than at me, he said, "Ma'am, you don't have to walk with him every day. He can walk with me."

I had seen this little boy every morning at the bus stop and had met his parents in passing. He really was a good child so I agreed and stood at my apartment building and watched their backs as they headed to the bus stop.

I set my class schedule according to Jaylan's school schedule so that I was in school when he was and back home before him, and I worked a few hours on my internship in between classes. In the afternoon, I watched from my balcony for the boys to head back towards the apartment. When he made it inside, we did his homework together then I let him play outside while I started my own homework.

Some evenings I had organizational meetings where I took Jaylan with me, and some evenings I had class and my cousin that lived in the dorm served as my sitter for a couple of hours. When I didn't have those obligations, we spent the evenings walking around the lake in our apartment complex where we fed the ducks. Jaylan was not much higher off the ground than the ducks so one time as he stuck out his little hand to offer a duck a piece of bread, the duck's beak engulfed his entire hand. Other ducks honked and rushed over for bread too. With one duck biting his hand and all the commotion from the others, Jaylan was scared. I picked up my baby and quickly headed back home. We didn't feed the ducks again for a long time after that. These walks to the lake were our time. No one and nothing else mattered.

After partaking in a simple dinner and hearing about the kids at school, we wound down for the night. Our routine was set, and bath time was followed by preparing clothes for the next day then reading.

Usually reading a children's Bible and other children's books, I read to Jaylan and over time he began to read to me. Pointing to the pictures and asking a million questions, he usually ensured we never finished an entire story. However, I was happy he was interested and engaged.

"Ah...Ah...Ah...pull," he sounded out the word "apple".

When he started reading to me, I was still pleased with his progress but my impatience with telling him how to pronounce the same word ten times made reading time a challenge for me. Closing my eyes, I silently asked God, "Lord, please give me the patience I need to not only teach my son to read, but also to be a good mother and endure all the challenges that are sure to come."

While we read, the stories were often interrupted with Jaylan's need to continue sharing the details of his adventurous day at school. Starting the moment he walked in the house from school and continuing until he was asleep, he explained who liked whom, who made a bad grade, what books they read, who said something funny, and much more than I ever cared to know. Exhausted from my long day, I usually did not feel like listening or responding, but I did.

"Ma, you know what? Mrs. Mason said I was the best one in the class today?" he started back.

"Oh, yeah? That's great!"

"And you know what else? Joshua said he doesn't want to be my friend anymore."

"Why is that?"

"I don't know. I don't like him anymore anyway. Michael is my friend though. You know, Michael?"

"Um, no. I haven't met Michael."

"Ma, what does lo-loquacious mean? 'Cause Mrs. Mason said April is that. Does it mean ugly?"

Laughing, I replied, "No, baby. It means she talks a lot. Well, it's time for you to go to sleep now. Let's say our prayers."

"Now I lay me down to sleep, I pray the Lord my soul to keep...," kneeled on the side of his bed, we said our prayers in unison.

In the years that followed, he proudly graduated to the Lord's Prayer, and we still said it together. Although he said his prayers with me, his information sharing shrunk. I regretted not taking more time to entertain his conversations. I was just tired. I was exhausted-physically, mentally, and emotionally, but I couldn't let it show.

Once I finally got him headed to the land of nod, I finished my own homework before sleeping for a few hours to prepare to do it all over the next day.

Lessons Learned:

♥ **Children grow up very fast.** I spent nine months afraid to see my baby, afraid to be a mother and afraid to do it alone. Before I knew it, my baby was no longer a baby. He was in school and had his own identity. I was still afraid and would be in a lot of ways for a long time, but each year was different and I learned a little more about my child and myself as we both grew together.

♥ **Whether it's time or money, my best investment was my son.** Regardless of the schedule for the day or the night, I made sure I did homework with Jaylan and read with him. I definitely didn't do everything right, but I always did my best.

Another Finish Line

For I can do everything through Christ, who gives me strength. -Philippians 4:13

My senior year was the culmination of all my hard work for the past four years and the spring board for the rest of my life. I stayed up late almost every night doing homework and completing the requirements for my bachelor's degree. The three years before had been challenging to say the least, but they had also been fun. Going into college, I had planned to get everything from the college experience that I could. Never once did I feel that I had sacrificed my job as a mother to do it. I had grown and learned a lot, and I did it as a mother. I did it *with* my son.

When I got stressed out with homework or with being a mother for all the various reasons as I often did, I pictured how much easier my life would be if it were normal. I imagined not having to go to class or do homework or be a mother at all let alone all by myself. There were many times that I wanted to give up. I often thought about moving back to Jackson where Jaylan and I could live with my grandmother and I wouldn't have to worry about paying bills and I would always have a babysitter.

Then I thought about all the people I knew, the decisions they made and the type of life those decisions had given them. I decided to sacrifice and work hard early in my life so that I could have a better life for my son later. I had endured four years of college and enjoyed my experience tremendously in spite of the challenges and was even rewarded for doing what I wanted to do anyway.

In my last year of college, I received three honors that I never dreamt I could achieve. I never even set them as goals. Going to college, doing my best, and graduating so that I could get a good job to support my son were my objectives. However, awards were nice.

In the fall of each year, the campus chapter of my sorority selected five local women to honor for achievement in various aspects identified as pertinent to the sorority on a national level. Four women with developed careers and one college student, usually from another college, were selected as award recipients.

Since I had been involved in the sorority, the student recipient was never one of our own members. That year, to my surprise, my chapter had chosen me to receive the award for the college student who had made significant contributions to the campus and to the community.

As I walked onto the stage to receive the award, I thought back to awards day in high school when my name was overlooked, when I missed my chance to stand up and show everyone that in spite of having a child I was still going to college and on a full scholarship. Standing behind the podium at the center of the stage with my plaque in hand, I looked down at the large, round table where Jaylan sat with my closest sorority sisters who had been like aunts to him. The smile in my heart manifested as a smile on my face, tears in my eyes, and a lump in my throat. My words were few, but my gratitude was huge.

Yes, Jaylan was with me at the ceremony. He was with me while I worked hard representing my sorority in meetings, community service, and on campus. Although he didn't fully understand why I was being recognized, he showed his pride in me with a big hug and a kiss on the cheek as I returned to the table.

The spring brought two more honors and even greater surprises for me. Sitting in my apartment going through the mail one day, I opened a letter from the University of Memphis's Fogelman College of Business. The letter stated that I had been selected as the business school's undergraduate marketing management major of the year. I didn't even know that such an award existed, and I certainly didn't expect to be the one to receive it. Although I made good grades in my classes, I was certain that I did not have the highest grade point average in my graduating class. I wondered, *How was I selected for this honor? Is this real?*

I never found out how I was chosen so I just thanked God for the honor and the much-needed monetary gift that came with it. Dressed in a cranberry red suit and black pumps that my internship manager had bought me as early graduation gifts, I attended the awards ceremony. Presenting me with the award was none other than Dr. Carson who had embraced me and my son as we began our journey at the university and given me some advice that I never forgot.

"Summer, as parents, we tend to either overdo it or under do it. Work hard to find the right balance."

I increasingly understood his advice each year as I faced the new challenges that came with my growing son and at the program that day, I was just thankful for another accomplishment with my child by my side. Dawning khaki pants and a collared shirt, Jaylan reached up and wrapped his little arms around my neck as I kneeled down. I always had the best date to all my functions.

The final honor I received as a University of Memphis student topped every award or recognition I had ever received and even made up for any I didn't get. In fact, it was the most prestigious award any female student could receive, Miss University of Memphis. Although I thought it was a bit ambitious of me to think that I could win, I had learned to always at least try. Sometimes I succeeded, and sometimes I didn't, but I felt good knowing that I tried.

In my four years at the university and through the organizations I had been involved in, I had the opportunity to exhibit everything they were asking for on the application. Simply being an active member of many organizations covered campus involvement. My sorority involvement was primarily about community involvement which included tutoring and coordinating activities at our adopted elementary school and at a nearby nursing home. Studying hard and maintaining high academic standards had earned me a cumulative 3.79 grade point average in my senior year including honors classes in my major. Finally, my scholarship program had encouraged and developed my leadership skills. On paper at least, I felt like I had it covered. However, the reality was that there were several other students who could tout the same thing. Many of them were my friends I had met throughout my college career and some I even met as early as Frosh Camp and orientation.

About two weeks after turning in my application, I received a letter notifying me that I was selected as one of the top five candidates and that I would be notified of my interview date and time. I could not believe it. I knew many of the people who had applied because people were talking about it, but I did not tell anyone that I had even applied. I wanted to minimize the embarrassment of applying and not winning. However, I had made it to the top five. Honestly, that was good enough for me. I was proud to say that, and I did. Letting my friends and family know that I was a finalist, I asked them to pray for me as I prepared for my interview.

Walking into the student government office in a dark tan suit I found at a discount store and the only pair of pumps I owned, I chose a seat in the empty holding room and waited for my name to be called. After only a few minutes, the student government president greeted me. "Hi, Summer. You ready to come on back?"

"Sure," I nervously replied. Entering the room, I was surprised to see the long conference table filled with familiar faces that represented each of the major organizations on campus. Each person had a vote and played a key role in determining who would win the coveted title. For a moment, I felt like I had an advantage because I knew each one of my questioners, but I quickly surmised that each of the candidates knew each of the questioners just as well or better than I did. They each asked various questions about my experiences at the university. I answered to the best of my ability and walked out of the interview knowing I had done my best. I was unsure of the outcome, but I was just thankful I had made the top five. The names of the winners were announced at the homecoming football game the following weekend.

At halftime of the game, the ten finalists for the titles of Mr. and Miss University of Memphis were escorted onto the middle of the long field. For what seemed like an eternity, I stood side by side with some of the greatest students at the school. All eyes in the stadium were on us, and being the only black student out of the ten, I stood out even more than the others.

One by one, our names were called as the finalists for the titles, and then my name was called again. It took a minute for it to register that Summer Curteece Owens had just been announced to the entire packed stadium as Miss University of Memphis. Although there was disappointment from the crowd for those who did not win, I heard a few cheers for me. I thought as we left the field, *Is this real? I can't believe it! I did it!*

Looking up at the jumbotron, I saw my face and thought about just how good God had been to me. As I made my way off the field, I was greeted by my number one fan, Jaylan, and some of my sorority sisters.

"Mommy, I saw you up there!" Jaylan exclaimed pointing up at the jumbotron, "Your head was so big!"

I laughed and embraced my baby.

"Now that's what I'm talking about! I knew you could do it, Summer," one of my friends shouted as she hugged me.

My parents weren't there that night, but that was my fault. Although I told them I had made it to the top five, I felt like that was as far as I would go in the competition. I didn't think I was going to win, and I did not want either of them to make the drive to Memphis to see me lose. But I did win. Summer Curteece Owens, who had a fatherless baby at fifteen years old was Miss University of Memphis. God was patting me on my back for working so hard all of those years, and he allowed me to enjoy it with the one who so many people thought would keep me from it.

My hard work had paid off, and I was soon the owner of my very first degree. Almost exactly four years from the date that I completed high school, I graduated from college. Approaching my twenty-second birthday, memories of seven years ago rushed through my head as they had done for the last few years. However, I pushed those thoughts aside to focus on another commencement ceremony. My college graduation was the end of my college career and the true beginning of my adult life.

The big day finally arrived. Because I had received the honor of being named Miss University of Memphis, I was given four tickets for reserved seats in the lowest section in the

Pyramid arena where the ceremony was held. These seats were only a few rows up from where I was sitting on the arena floor.

Before I got in line for the processional, my dad and stepmother surprisingly presented me with graduation gifts, "Summer, we're so proud of you. Here, put these on."

Opening a little black, velvet box, I found a pair of diamond earrings. I clinched my graduation cap between my knees which were lost beneath the big, royal blue gown and placed the earring in the holes in my ears and screeched a loud thank you as I wrapped my arms around my dad's neck.

"There's one more," my dad continued handing me a long flat box covered like the earring box.

It was a diamond tennis bracelet. I had never gotten gifts that nice before, and I was nervous that I might lose them during the ceremony.

"Okay, you keep this for now," I insisted handing him back the tennis bracelet, "I'll just wear the earrings today. Thank you sooooooooo much!" I kissed him on the cheek and ran to join my classmates in line preparing to march to our seats.

Pomp and Circumstance played as we strutted in proudly reflecting on our separate but united journeys towards our bachelor's degrees. Once we were seated, I scanned the audience for my little cheering section. Although there were over 10,000 people in attendance, my parents and my son were seated at what seemed like only an arms-length away from me. A little further up were my sisters and brothers, GG, a couple of uncles and some cousins. I was happy and thankful they had taken the time to support me that day and throughout my life. I snuck in a wave and a huge smile to them and refocused my attention on the speaker.

Each school of the university was called up, and row by row the line of students approached the stage. Each student's name was called and he or she walked across the stage, moved their tassels to the right side of the cap then stopped at the end to take a very quick photo and headed back to the seats. After what seemed like hours, the business school was directed to advance to the stage.

As I walked towards the stage with my row, I gave my family another glance and a huge buck-toothed smile that I no longer was ashamed to show. Almost my turn to accept my degree, I nervously watched the students in front of me climb the stairs and float across the stage. Because the president of the university had just retired, an interim president distributed the diplomas and shook our hand as we crossed the stage and officially became alumnae. Finally, "Sum-mer Cur-teece O-wens" was spoken slowly and loudly over the microphone. I took a deep breath and, concentrating on each step, proudly yet shyly walked across the stage with my red honor cord and AKA cloth around my neck. I grabbed my degree cover, shook the interim president's hand, moved my tassel to the right side of my cap as I had done four years ago at my high school graduation, walked down the few steps on the side of the stage and smiled for the photo that was taken on the count of one. I graduated magna cum laude and even almost earned summa cum laude distinction.

Leaving the arena, we headed to an apartment clubhouse that Chinitra and I rented for a joint post-graduation celebration with our family and friends. Chinitra had started the journey with me as little girls, and we finished together as women. We both had our parents, siblings and cousins, as well as our sorority sisters, in attendance so we packed the clubhouse. Talking, laughing, dancing and remembering the events of the past four years of college and even the years before since Chinitra and I had been friends since third grade, we relished in our accomplishments. At the end of the night, we cut the huge, white sheet cake outlined with pink roses and green ivy leaves and decorated with a photo of Chinitra and me in the center. I gave my six-year-old son, a big piece of cake and an even bigger kiss and thanked God again for bringing us so far together.

Lessons Learned:

♥ **Anything is possible.** When I wasn't even expected to graduate from high school, I did. I went on to college and did everything I would have done had I not been a teenage mother. I did it with my son by my side and maybe even because of him. God showed me that all I had to do was put forth the effort and He would bless me with the beautiful outcome.

♥ **Don't waste time on trivial things.** My time was focused on bettering myself and helping my son. No matter how hard it got or when I felt like giving up, I knew I could not. A little sacrifice of my time and having fun with my friends and a lot of hard work in high school and college had already paid off and that was just the beginning.

The Real World

God is with you in all that you do. -Genesis 21:22

I had graduated from college and was on the hunt for a job. I had a great resume that included good grades, internship experience and campus involvement, and I thought employers would be knocking down my door to hire me. However, I was unpleasantly surprised.

I graduated with a Bachelor's of Business Administration degree in marketing and wanted to work in marketing, promotions, public relations, or advertising. While interning in the corporate office of the hotel chain where I worked for three years in the marketing department, at my supervisor's recommendation, I took a week away from my role to spend time in a local hotel cross-training in the various areas of hotel operations. During that week, I spent a day at the front desk, a day in housekeeping, a day shadowing the general manager, and two days with the sales department-one in the office and one in the field.

I learned a lot from the experience, but one of the main things I learned was that I did not want to work in sales. I only wanted to work in marketing. For this reason, when I was offered a job as a sales executive for the hotel branch in Nashville, I quickly denied the opportunity saying, "Thanks, but no thanks." With my credentials, I was sure I would be able to find another job doing what I really wanted to do.

I ended up spending the next two months bargaining for a babysitter for Jaylan, putting on my navy blue interview suit that had been purchased for me by my supervisor when I was an intern, going to interviews when I could get one, and coming home disappointed or hoping for that call with a job offer that never came. As the summer progressed and the days got closer to the start of a new school year for Jaylan, I had to figure out what I was going to do and where I was going to live.

Rent was still due each month, and money was running out. Our lease was ending soon, and my roommate, Chinitra, and I didn't know if we should or could even afford to renew it. We were scared, frustrated and even a bit depressed. Unsure of what to do if I couldn't find a job, I contemplated moving back to Jackson to live with my grandmother. I wondered, *Alright, here we go. Is now the time that I have to give up and move back home? I've come so far. Can I please find a job to take care of my son?*

Finally, things began to look up. I had been interviewing with a prominent rental car company and was on my fourth and final interview. Each interview was with someone higher up in the company, and I had been told by others working in the company that once I made it through the fourth interview I was going to get a job offer. At the same time, I was interviewing with a small advertising agency and had been called in for a second interview. The job at the advertising agency was exactly what I wanted to do, and I would be able to create marketing campaigns and develop collateral for different companies. Although more operational, the rental car job included some marketing elements and had a clearly defined path for promotion.

After my fourth interview, I was offered the job at the rental car company which presented a dilemma. I expressed my appreciation for the job offer and asked when they needed a final answer of acceptance. Because I figured I would enjoy the ad agency job more, I wanted to see if I would get an offer from that company before accepting the other offer. I was given five days to respond, and the next day I did get an offer from the advertising agency. With two job offers, I was excited about finally getting a job. However, I had a decision to make. Which job should I select?

Positive and negative points existed for both positions, but the rental car company paid more, offered health insurance and offered better growth opportunities. My choice was clear so I called only two days after getting the offer to accept and find out when I would start.

"Hi, this is Summer Owens. May I speak with Mr. Johnson?"

A cold, monotone female voice on the other end of the phone replied, "Ms. Owens, this is Catherine Smith, his assistant. He asked me to let you know that we've decided to pursue other candidates." I was too shocked to ask any questions and just gave a confused,

"Um. Okay...?" and hung up the phone.

When the shock wore off a few minutes later, I couldn't believe that I did not ask how they could take the job away from me after offering it to me and giving me time to consider the offer. I had already declined the offer at the advertising agency so I was back at square one with no job and a child to figure out how to support.

I thought, *You big dummy. You should have just taken the job in the first place. You know people who work there, and they like it. You would have liked it too, but no. Now, you have nothing. What are you gonna do now? Huh?*

Our apartment lease ended, and no new money was coming into the house. After her unsuccessful attempts at securing a job in Memphis, Chinitra moved to Washington, DC with another friend who had gotten a job there. With Chinitra leaving and me not having a job, the only solution I came up with was to move back to Jackson and live with my grandmother until I could find a job. I had to do something.

I really didn't want to move back home though. Still pondering other options, I decided to go back to school and pursue my MBA since I knew I eventually wanted to earn it anyway. I no longer had a scholarship, but as a student I could secure student loans to cover my tuition and help with my living expenses. I hated borrowing money especially when I had to pay interest, but I was left with few choices and this one kept me from relying on my family and would position me for an advanced degree. I patted myself on the back, *Good thinking. Glad I came up with this. How bad would it look to finally get a degree and still have to move home?*

I temporarily moved into Bilicia's one bedroom apartment. I made the difficult decision to send Jaylan to Jackson while I sorted out our next steps. Making Bilicia's living room my bedroom, I prepared to take the GMAT, the entrance exam for business school. After taking the test, all I could do was wait on the results. However, while I was waiting, God was working something else out for me. One day when I was with Bilicia at her aunt's house, her aunt asked me if I had heard the rumors that the Vancouver Grizzlies, a National Basketball Association team, was considering relocating to Memphis. I had not heard the rumors, but I dreamily stated, "Wow, it would be great to work in marketing for them." The next day when I was in Jackson visiting Jaylan at my mother's house, I got on her computer and found the team's website. No jobs were listed as the team had not confirmed whether or not it would relocate to Memphis, but I saw where I could sign up to be notified when jobs were posted to the site.

A couple of weeks after signing up for the notification, the team officials announced they had chosen Memphis as the team's new home. Almost immediately following the announcement, I received an email with information about interviews for account manager positions that were being held downtown. Although these were four-month temporary sales positions, I thought to myself, *This might be my way to get my foot in the door.*

Back in my navy blue interview suit and praying as I drove, I headed downtown and entered a packed hotel ballroom full of people interested in the posted positions. The huge group of candidates was then divided into smaller groups of about fifteen people and directed to separate rooms. In my group, we handed our resumes to the two gentlemen facilitating the interview and were seated around a huge conference room table. One by one, we introduced ourselves and tried to sell ourselves for the sales position with the team. I was the youngest and most inexperienced person in the room, but I did my best to convey confidence in myself and stated that I gave 100% to anything I did and had never allowed myself to fail.

Next, I expected to get a typical interview question like, "Tell us how you handled a situation where...". However, we were not asked any questions and were excused after only giving our personal sales pitch. Something I said worked because I was invited to the second round of interviews.

The second interview was one-on-one with a professional from the Grizzlies organization, and God was smiling on me when He paired me with the human resources director for the team. During my interview, we talked about my background and experience, which were good for my age but extremely limited especially in the area of sales. I don't remember what question she asked or how the next topic came up because she legally could not ask about my family situation, and I never planned to reveal that I was a single mother in an interview. Knowing that most companies probably wouldn't prefer to hire someone in my situation, I wanted to keep that my secret at least until I got the job. However, somehow we ended up discussing the fact that I was a single mother. So was she. She said she admired me for what I had accomplished as a single mother and thought I would be great for the job. I was hired as an account manager with the Memphis Grizzlies.

Although it was a short-term position, I moved out of Bilicia's apartment and into my own one-bedroom apartment in the same complex. Jaylan and I shared a bedroom again, but the small apartment was all we needed to get us started through the next phase of our lives. Although I had taken the GMAT to attend business school, graduate school would have to wait while I started my career.

Lessons Learned:

♥ **Sometimes our biggest disappointments are our greatest blessings.** After I was told by the rental car company that I no longer had the job offer they had extended to me, I was distraught. However, once I got the job with the Grizzlies I thanked God for keeping me from the rental car company. Had I been working for the rental car company, I would never have pursued a job with the Grizzlies.

♥ **What God has for me, it is for me.** The team was looking for the best sales people in Memphis to get the team started, and I was certainly not one of them. However, I was one of the people hired for the job which was my first job out of college. By working hard in college, I had positioned myself to be ready for the opportunity when it came my way.

You Better Work

Work willingly at whatever you do, as though you were working for the Lord rather than for people. Remember that the Lord will give you an inheritance as your reward, and that the Master you are serving is Christ. -Colossians 3:23-24

After thinking I would not find a job, I was blessed with a job with the most exciting event happening in town at the time- the arrival of an NBA team. Ironically, I was employed as an account executive, a sales representative, which was exactly the position I had declined with the hotel company.

Although the title was the same, I knew the job would be different. Unlike the hotel business, the NBA team was new and intriguing and everyone wanted to be a part of it. Always exciting, my job was fast-paced and fascinating and there was basically no competition for the ticket packages I sold. Yes, I was a salesperson, but this was nothing like what I would have done with any other company.

I was young and energetic, ready and willing to work all night as was often required to get the team ready to start the season. However, unlike most of my co-workers, I was a single mother with a young child. Each morning, I walked Jaylan to his bus stop in the front of our new apartment complex and usually waited with him for the bus before rushing to work downtown where I would be late into the night.

My sorority sister, Aimee, lived relatively close to my new apartment so she agreed to pick Jaylan up from his after school program and take him to her house until I got off work whenever I worked late. She helped him with his homework and made sure he was fed. Because he was usually asleep by the time I got to Aimee's house, I usually slung his backpack over my shoulder, picked up my growing little man laying his head on my shoulder, and carried his dead weight out to the car. When we got back to my apartment, I lugged him up to our third floor apartment. I felt guilty being away from him and needing

122

someone else to help him with homework and feed him. Some days I wondered, *Should I look for another job where I can work normal hours? This isn't fair to my baby. What else can I do?* My internal torment persisted, but I knew the long hours were only temporary and would pay off for us eventually.

Adding to my suffering, the sales job got more difficult, and I began to pursue a marketing position which was the main reason I accepted the sales position with the Grizzlies. I had my foot in the door, and I planned to get the rest of my body in too. During my internship, my supervisor purchased a leather portfolio for me to use to display and present my work during interviews. Since then I had been building a portfolio with materials including fliers, newsletters, press releases, photos, and other items demonstrating my marketing experience while in college and during my internship. I was ready to share my portfolio with the right person at the Grizzlies to get me in marketing.

I watched the team website for job postings like the rest of the community and many people in other markets who were looking for their big break into sports. When I saw three open marketing positions, I quickly composed cover letters for each one. Handing them, along with my resume, to both the director of promotions who was hiring a promotions coordinator and to the director of marketing who was hiring an administrative assistant and a marketing coordinator, I felt like I was finally making progress towards my goal.

After reviewing my resume, the director of promotions informed me that I wasn't a good fit for her open position; however, I still had not heard back from the marketing director, Marla. The team was still operating on a barebones crew with only the few employees who had moved to Memphis from Vancouver along with the sales team and a few others who had been hired since the move. The marketing department consisted only of the director and a graphic designer, and everyone was extremely busy. Not wanting to ruin my chances of getting a position by annoying Marla, I waited for what I felt was the right opportunity to approach her.

Gathering my nerves and clinching my portfolio, I asked her if she had received my cover letter and resume applying for her marketing coordinator position. She gave me a smile that I couldn't decipher as real or fake and replied, "Yes, I received it, but I have been extremely busy."

"I certainly understand. I just wanted to give you this as well to take a look at if you have a free moment," I said sitting the packed portfolio on her desk. I continued, "It's my portfolio, and it may help you visualize what I've written in the resume. I really appreciate your consideration."

"Thanks. I'll look at it when I can," she replied as she turned back towards her computer.

She was not mean, but she certainly was not inviting either so I kept my interaction with her to a minimum but frequent enough to ensure she didn't forget about me. I was very nervous, but I was proud that I made that step verbally expressing my interest in her position.

Still not hearing back from Marla, the four-month temporary account executive assignment with the team quickly came to an end. Of the twenty-five account executives hired, the sales managers hired only eight of us as permanent employees with the team. I had fared better than I thought I would in sales, but my co-workers were just much better sales people.

On the gloomy day when we found out which of us would be unemployed again, we all sat waiting in our open work area as we were summoned back one by one. I wasn't expecting to stay anyway, but I didn't know what I'd do without a job. As I continued waiting on my turn to be released from the team and returned to unemployment, I completely tuned out everything around me. I even stopped noticing when the other sales people came out of the conference room.

Hoping and praying that I would be asked to stay on with the team even if it was in sales, I just needed an income to support my son and myself. I thought, *What will I do? Will I be able to find another job? How will I pay my bills? Will I have to break my lease and move back to Jackson after all? Should I go back to school now and live off of loan money? If I don't have a job, I can't keep my apartment. Then I'll have to move and Jaylan will have to change schools. How will I tell him he has to leave his friends just because I can't find a job?*

When it was almost my turn to enter the conference room to receive my fate, Marla discreetly slid an envelope towards me and kept walking. I immediately turned towards the cubicle wall beside me to inconspicuously open the envelope. Covering my mouth with my hand and looking around to see if anyone was watching me, I released an internal shout of joy. I held in my shaking hands an offer letter to be Marla's marketing assistant. The salary for the position was about the same small amount as what I'd been offered by the advertising agency, but that was more than the zero dollars I would have otherwise had. I was thankful to have a permanent job. And, best of all, I would be in marketing.

As if she could read my mind, Marla explained the next day that she felt I was overqualified to be her administrative assistant yet not quite qualified enough to be a marketing coordinator. Combining the two positions, she made me her marketing assistant. I was fine with that. I was just thankful to have a job, and the added benefit was that I was out of sales and into marketing. I was thankful Marla was taking a chance on me, but I was afraid of how I would continue to balance the hectic schedule of continuing to work for a sports team with being a single mother. Also, the yearly salary I earned as a marketing assistant was less than what I earned in four months of working in sales so I had to tighten my budget even more. I gladly did, and I felt in my heart that this was just the beginning. God was going to see to it that I had a great career that would benefit Jaylan and me in many ways too.

After only a few months as a marketing assistant, I received a promotion to marketing coordinator. Although my pay didn't increase, I was thankful for the consideration of the title change. As a marketing assistant, I was doing the work outlined in the marketing coordinator job description and had proven I was ready for the position and the title. Even though I was disappointed that I didn't get the desperately needed raise, I believed that if I was faithful and diligent and continued to do the best work I could then the pay would soon follow. And it did.

Eventually, I received a raise of $125 a month which was small but enough to cover a bill or go into savings. It was also enough to allow me to sign Jaylan up for the karate classes he had been asking to start. Getting him to those classes was a regular challenge, but at least I could afford them. That's all I could ask for at the time, and I was thankful for the steps I was taking to move forward no matter how small.

Lessons Learned:

- ♥ **Someone's always watching so give them something to see.** The entire company was watching all the sales representatives considering us for various positions throughout the company. If I had not given my job in sales my best effort, I likely would have never been hired in marketing.

- ♥ **Make the sacrifice.** I knew my sacrifices then would one day mean that my son and I could have everything we needed and most of what we wanted.

- ♥ **Keep moving forward.** Constantly, setting new goals for myself kept me motivated to continue getting better. As long as I took one step forward, I would eventually reach every goal I set for myself no matter how unattainable it may seem.

- ♥ **It's not all about the money.** Accepting my marketing position, I didn't earn nearly the amount of money I thought I deserved. However, I had a job. Even when I got my promotion to marketing coordinator, I still wasn't paid what thought I would with my college degree. However, I was learning, developing and progressing.

Not a Baby Anymore

Direct your children onto the right path, and when they are older, they will not leave it. - Proverbs 22:6

Aimee continued to pick Jaylan up from school for me on nights I had to work late for games. As an employee, I received a pair of season tickets and on occasion, Aimee and other friends picked Jaylan up from school and brought him to games. I was thankful to have the tickets for my son to enjoy the games and as a form of payment to my friends for keeping him. Having him at the arena made it easier and faster for me to get him home at night and in bed to rest before school the next day.

It was at school that he got to see other children and how they lived and how our two-person family was different. As Jaylan progressed through school balancing work and life as a single mother got a little easier because I was getting used to it; however, answering his questions got harder. Being around his classmates and seeing their parents made him wonder about his own situation. Then one day while he was in the second grade, I got the question I had been dreading and avoiding since the day he was born. Although I'm sure she had good intentions, his teacher sent home an assignment that was probably easy for most of the other students in Jaylan's class to complete. However, for my child, it only brought out questions and confusion that I was not ready to handle.

On an 8 1/2 x 11 inch sheet of white typing paper was a large outline of a tree that took up the entire page. In the middle of the page, just above the trunk was a line filled in with Jaylan's name. Branched out above his name were lines for "Mother's name" to the right and "Father's name" to the left.

When we sat down to do homework, Jaylan quickly filled in my name. Then he turned to me and asked, "Ma, what am I supposed to write here?" as he pointed to the line that read "Father's name".

"Um, baby. Why don't you write Granddaddy's name?" After all, my dad was the closest thing to a father to my baby. But that was not good enough for my inquisitive child. He wanted to know more.

He continued, "But Ma, that's your daddy...not mine, right?"

He was very smart, and I often found myself and others talking to him more like an adult than a child. However, I needed God to give me the words to say to him at this moment. I prayed, *Lord, please guide me. Show me how to tell my baby why he doesn't have his own father's name to write in that blank. I just don't know what to say.*

Although it may have been premature for my elementary school student, I proceeded to reveal the truth to him.

"Okay, baby. Let me try to explain it to you. When a man and a woman are married and love each other they do something and make a baby. Like your friend Michael has a mommy and a daddy, but sometimes it doesn't happen like that. One day a man that I didn't know did to me what makes a woman have a baby. Then I had you, and I get to be your mommy *and* your daddy. And you know what..."

"What?" his eyes widened as he asked.

"God is my daddy and yours too, and he's going to take care of us," I stated as I continued tickling his stomach.

Before he was even born, I felt guilty that my son didn't have a father, but after that conversation I felt even worse. I don't know if my answer to his question helped him or confused him even more, but the questions went away for a while, and so did my frustration towards the teacher who gave him the family tree assignment. Surely, I was not the only single mother of the class. Looking at the sweet, little face that once lived inside of me, I was tormented knowing that he did not have a man to help him become a man. He only had me to throw the ball with him and help him with his homework. Only me to talk to him about girls and sex and to teach him how to drive. Only me to reward him, encourage him, love him and discipline him. I prayed for God to help me raise my son.

We did math homework and science homework, but no assignments were tougher for me than the family tree, but soon the family tree was behind us, and we pressed on. With a slight salary increase, I analyzed my budget and decided to pursue the dream I'd had since I entered the workforce; to buy a house. To some people, the goal seemed unreasonable, but I knew anything was possible. Although it wasn't the biggest or the nicest, the house I grew up in was my home. We had a front yard and backyard to play in and tiny rooms packed with our large family, but it was ours. I wanted my son to have a house to call home too.

Lessons Learned:

- ♥ **Get ready to answer the tough questions.** Catching me off guard, my son asked me a question I wasn't prepared to answer. That experience taught me that I would not get to choose when the questions would come or what they would be but I needed to be prepared with a response.

- ♥ **Keep setting new goals.** Someone once said success is not a quick trip, it is a journey. When I finished college, my goal was to get a full-time, permanent job. I did, and then I wanted to be promoted. I was. God positions us to take steps, sometimes small and sometimes large ones, to make each of our goals attainable.

The Next Big Thing

You don't have enough faith," Jesus told them. "I tell you the truth, if you had faith even as small as a mustard seed, you could say to this mountain, 'Move from here to there,' and it would move. Nothing would be impossible. -Matthew 17:20

Although I was still living on a meager salary, I wanted to do something big for my baby. I wanted to fulfill the American dream and buy a house. *Are you crazy? You know you can't afford a house. You need to just keep renting.* I was sure my own thoughts mirrored those who knew how much money I made, but I was determined to own my own home.

I didn't know the first thing about buying a house though. My parents both owned houses, but they had never said anything to me about owning a house myself. I didn't know where to start so I turned to the internet. I began to learn about first-time home buyer programs, loans, and what to look for when evaluating houses and began evaluating my options. I also began saving money for my first house.

As a temporary employee of the Grizzlies, I shared with one of my co-workers that one day I wanted to own my own home. We both laughed knowing the insufficient pay I earned and the fact that it was likely that I wouldn't even have a job in a few months. "Summer, are you kidding? You must be talking about in a few years. You know we don't make enough money for that." However, I was serious.

"No, as soon as I get a permanent job no matter how much I make," I insisted.

"Okay, miss lady. Do it then," was the challenge issued to me. His disbelief in me made me even more determined to pay a mortgage rather than rent.

As soon as I was hired into the marketing department, I set up a savings account at a credit union with an automatic deposit of $100 from every paycheck. The credit union had only two branches that were far away from my job making it difficult for me to access the money which was what I wanted so that I couldn't transfer money into my checking account or make withdrawals easily. Barely making enough money to pay my bills, it was a huge sacrifice for me. After that money was taken off the top, I still had to pay rent, my car note, utility bill, and other living expenses. I really didn't think I had money to spare, but I was determined to start saving something. Not knowing how much the house would cost or how much I would have to pay upfront, I didn't have a specific goal amount in mind. I just wanted to save as much as I could, and the best way for me to do that was to have it come out of my paycheck before I could even see it. Quickly, I adjusted to living off of less money and increased my savings, even if it was only by a few dollars, every few months.

Increasing my direct deposits was not the only method employed to save money, I used every technique I could think of to save as much money as I could as fast as I could. The major thrust in my "Jaylan and Summer's house" account came when I received my income tax return. Because my salary was so low, I did not pay a lot of money in taxes. However, my return ended up being higher because I was able to benefit from the earned income tax credit. My low income actually worked in my favor. Without a second thought, I deposited the entire check into the account for our first house. Many people I knew would spend their refund checks on new cars, clothes or other things that were soon inoperable or were just pretty meaningless. Or the money would be spent in a hundred different places on a hundred different things to the point where once it was all gone, they would wonder what they had gotten with it. Not me. That lump sum was put towards something that would make a major difference in my life. I did not spend a dime of it on clothes for me or even for Jaylan. No, he did not get new Jordan's like other children his age, and I did not get my nails done or new outfit. Every penny of it went in the bank.

I took other money-saving measures too. I brought my lunch of frozen meals or ate leftovers most days rather than eating out at restaurants. Some days, I didn't eat lunch or just nibbled on crackers all day. I remembered my grandmother explaining, "Baby, eat your oatmeal so you won't be hungry. You know, it sticks to your bones." She was right. On days when I did not have leftovers from the night before, my oatmeal breakfast sustained me until I got home. Because of my limited earnings, Jaylan qualified for and received free lunch at school so he was not suffering as I sacrificed for our house.

My primary expenses were rent, utilities, car note, child care and food, and I stretched every dime I made. Investing in three pairs of nice $20 slacks and a couple of shirts and mixing and matching them so people did not notice that I was wearing the same things all the time, I did not need to buy any new clothes. Regular hair appointments which were already infrequent were eliminated. Part of me cared what people thought, but a bigger part of me knew that it did not matter. I had bigger plans and one day I would be able to buy anything I wanted.

The money in the savings account added up even faster than I thought it would. By the time I began to actually look at houses, I had close to $9,000 in the account. In the midst of my extreme savings, I was still doing research on how to actually buy a house. I had heard people in the past talk about first-time home buyer programs and read about some on the internet. I thought, *I'm so confused. Surely, I can find someone to help me. Am I in over my head? Maybe I should use that money for something else and just stay in my apartment. There's nothing wrong with it. There are so many loan types, and I have no idea which one I need? What's the deal with the interest rates, and what does prime mean anyway? When I think of points, I think of basketball. What are points for a mortgage?*

I found out that my mother had a friend who was a real estate agent, and she directed me to a loan program called NACA that made the journey to my dream a little easier. After signing up for the program and finding out the loan amount I qualified for, my real estate agent pulled a list of homes for sale in my price range that met my criteria.

Over several hot, summer days, my agent, my son and I visited houses. With my limited income, I was still determined to find a nice house in a safe area for a single mother and her young son in a good school district and with a reasonable commute to my job. I prayed for guidance and direction as I began to get frustrated thinking, *Will I ever find a house like I want? Lord, is this a sign that I can't afford what I want? Do I need to wait a few more years when maybe I'll earn more money and can get a higher loan?*

One day, while visiting a co-worker's home for the first time, I found what would soon be my new neighborhood. Most houses in the nice neighborhood had three bedrooms, two bathrooms and a garage, and it was only about a twenty minute commute downtown.

Excited about the possibility that I had another starting place to view houses, I said, "Well, that is good to hear. It seems nice over here. What about kids? Where do they go to school?"

"I hear the elementary school is nice, and it's right up the street," my co-worker and friend continued her sales pitch to make me her neighbor.

I told my agent that I had finally decided on the neighborhood where I wanted to live. All we had to do was find the right house.

My agent pulled a list of houses in that neighborhood and over the next few weeks she, Jaylan and I looked at every house on the market in that neighborhood. Drenched with sweat in the middle of a hot, Memphis summer, we entered house after house. By the end of the week, we had seen every vacant house in the neighborhood including the very last house in the entire subdivision which I selected. Nestled in a cove, the house had three bedrooms, two bathrooms, a garage, and it was vacant so I was able to move in as soon as my offer was accepted and the paperwork was done.

At closing, I signed all the paperwork making the house ours. The mortgage on my new house was only $100 more than I had been paying for rent in my one bedroom apartment. With the keys and garage door openers in hand, I strolled out of the office and headed straight to our new house, our new home. Jaylan had a backyard to play football with the friends he made after we moved into the neighborhood. We had a deck to host cookouts and relax on under the tall shade trees that looked over my house.

I took only a few days to get unpacked and somewhat settled and began to tackle my next issue. During the first few weeks in our new home, I was able to leave work early to pick him up from school. However, leaving work every day was not a feasible option for me. Finding an afterschool program for him to attend became a top priority. Although his new school did not have an afterschool program, the school partnered with organizations like the YMCA and local churches to provide aftercare. The problem for me was that I had begun my search too late, and all the programs were full. In my new house, I lived too far away from my friends who might be able to help me with Jaylan after school and on game nights. The only friend nearby was my co-worker Staci, but she worked when I worked so she couldn't help me either. My supervisor was very understanding, but her patience could only last so long. I had to be at work, but I had to pick up my son from school. I wondered, *What am I going to do? I wish my family was here to help me? Was it a mistake to move here where I have no help?*

By the third week of school, I still did not have a solution. Although my boss didn't like it, I continued leaving work to pick him up from school. Finally, one day as I was talking to my friend and former co-worker, Keyaschei, she mentioned that her baby was in a day care at a church that provided aftercare for my son's school. I responded, "Yeah, they were the first ones I called, but they are full too."

"Let me call them and see what I can do," she offered.

After explaining my situation to the director of the program and letting them know that we were friends, she called me with the response.

"Done. You can take him tomorrow!" Keyaschei exclaimed.

The next day I signed him up, and he rode the bus to his new afterschool program. He adjusted to the new school and afterschool program quickly. He was a very adaptable kid and dealt well with all the changes my life and my decisions brought to our lives.

Although Keyaschei lived a good distance away from me, Keyaschei lived much closer to me than any of my other friends.

She even ended up being my game night babysitter for a while. Driving to her house late at night after games, I woke up my sleeping son and headed home. I was thankful for my friend, and I was thankful for her help getting a place in the after school program.

The program was a Godsend for me and for my son. First of all, I was thankful just to have a place for my son to go after school. However, I was even more grateful that he was at a church every day after school. At the church, the student teachers ensured homework was completed and even helped them do it. Bible study for the students was held each Friday, and we enjoyed a discounted dinner with the members of the church some Wednesday nights.

On other nights of the week, Jaylan was involved in other activities I discovered to help him meet people in our new community, to become a more well-rounded individual and to just stay busy. Learning about a Cub Scouts group at his school, I signed him up.

"Ma, I don't think I'll like that. Do I have to? Well, what do they do? Will I have to wear that?" he frowned and motioned at the shirt of one of the young scouts attending the meeting with his father.

Walking away from him, he followed behind me still whining and asking questions as I turned in the registration sheet.

I finally responded to him trying to stay positive although I was frustrated with his negativity, "That's okay. We'll get to see. Let's just give it a try. I think you'll learn a lot and have a lot of fun."

I attended the first meeting with him, but by the second meeting he just wanted me to drop him. "I'm okay, Ma. You don't have to stay," he insisted. I headed home thankful for the opportunity to use that hour to myself.

Jaylan quickly befriended another scout whose father was a one of the Cub Scouts leaders. One of the nicest men I'd ever met, this married father of two began picking up my son for every meeting and bringing him back home. Giving Jaylan his first sleeping bag, his leader took Jaylan on his first camping trip.

Jaylan had made friends in the neighborhood, but he was doing Cub Scouts on his own. Watching him demonstrate how to tie a slip knot and hearing him talk about everything they'd done in the woods, I was assured that he was enjoying his new experience.

I was thankful for the leader who took care of Jaylan like his own son during Scout events even helping Jaylan carve the wood and build his car for the Cub Scouts annual Derby Days race. In the small building packed with Cub Scouts and their parents, Jaylan placed his little red car on the track and watched it fly by his competition. Leaving with a shiny, gold trophy in his hand, my proud little boy expressed his gratitude for me making him join the organization when he looked up at me smiling as he exclaimed with his mouth trying to keep pace with his thoughts, "I can't believe I won. I didn't think it would be fun, but it was. Ma, did you see how my car passed Josh's? And, Ma, did you see...?"

He continued talking as we walked to the car, as we drove home, and even as we walked into the house. I heard most of the words he said, but they all meant the same thing to me, "Thank you, Mama." That was all I needed to hear, and he told me in his own way.

After a couple of months I began to fall behind on payments for the afterschool program, but a gesture by the director of the program reminded me that God wouldn't let me fail. I had always done well at budgeting and saving my modest income, but I was challenged with making my new mortgage payments, paying other bills, trying to tithe, and covering the cost for the afterschool program alone. Although we still did not enjoy luxuries like cable, making ends meet was a daily struggle. The director of the afterschool program knew that I was a single mother and wanted to help me. "Summer, how are you doing?" the director asked.

"Um, I'm okay. How are you?" I replied.

"Thanks for the payment you made yesterday. You're all caught up now, but I have a question to ask you."

"Okay, sure. What is it?"

"You know we're not in business to make money, right?"

A bit confused, I responded, "Okay."

She continued, "We're here to provide care for children, not to make money. We just have to be able to pay our bills. If I cut the fee in half for you, would that work for you?"

Almost too emotional to respond, I slowly wrapped by arms around her hugging her like a mother and uttered, "Thank you so much."

By the time Jaylan was out of the program in fifth grade, I was earning more money and paid the church back the other half of the fee that had so generously been waived for me.

Extremely appreciative of the kind gesture of the afterschool program director, I was also hurt that I had to accept it. I was a college graduate with a full-time job but was still very limited financially. Although I thoroughly enjoyed my job, it took a lot of my time away from Jaylan and I still struggled financially. We had a comfortable home and a decent car, but I wanted to be able to do more for my son. I wanted to save for his college education and my own retirement. I thought, *How can I make more money? What else can I do? Should I look for another job because this isn't working?* I didn't have all the answers to my questions, but I knew I had to do something.

Lessons Learned:

♥ **Save something every month.** Open a savings account and make regular contributions to it. Even if it is only $5, save money for a rainy day. Save for a house. Save for college. Make sacrifices for the future. Watch the money grow and do something meaningful with it.

♥ **Home ownership is possible for everyone.** When I saved thousands of dollars to buy my first house, I was earning barely enough money to pay a modest rental fee. Through persistence, research, dedication, and education, I was able to buy *and afford* a beautiful home with all my specifications for more than my salary would have allowed.

♥ **Work hard, live right and the blessings will come.** When I was looking for someone to keep Jaylan for me, God sent an angel who got him into a wonderful program that I was unable to get him in myself.

Continuing Education

Commit your actions to the Lord, and your plans will succeed.
-Proverbs 16:3

I was excited about my new home, and I enjoyed my job. However, I still wanted more out of my life and my career. I had an undergraduate degree in marketing, but two years into my job I was still struggling financially. I pondered what I could do to make more money. Not only did I want to give myself more leverage for another promotion, but I also wanted the satisfaction of saying I had achieved the accomplishment of getting a masters degree. I was going back to school. Because the team offered tuition reimbursement and I had also taken out a loan, money was not the issue with me returning to school. It was time.

I faced a dilemma. How could I go to school, work a full time job that required sixty to eighty hours a week of my time, *and* manage as a full-time, single mother? I didn't know the answer, but I didn't waste time trying to figure it out. I knew whatever I came up with wouldn't make sense, and I would end up talking myself out of going back to school. I just began to look for a school that fit my needs as a working, single mother.

After about a month of online research and talking to friends, co-workers and former classmates, I found the perfect school for me. Offering bachelor's and master's degrees in various studies, Belhaven College was a Christian-based school that incorporated a Biblical worldview into each of its courses. My goal was to earn an MBA, Masters in Business Administration, degree and Belhaven offered an accelerated program where I could get it in eighteen months. Not disciplined enough for an online program, I resigned myself to the fact that I needed to be in a physical classroom. Belhaven was centrally located between my job downtown and my house so I could go straight to class from work.

Go straight to school from work? Wait a minute, how am I going to do that? What if I have to work a game? What am I going to do with Jaylan? Remembering my high school and undergraduate graduations and the events that led up to them, I knew I could do it. Shaking off the doubt, I finished the application and decided to let God show me the answers to my questions rather than worrying about them myself. Two years out of college, I was relieved I had already taken the GMAT when I was unable to find a job and thought my only option was to go right back to school. On the application was an essay question on why I should be selected for the program. The basis of my answer was my determination to succeed and excel in spite of any obstacles I faced.

Accepted into the program, I started classes before basketball season began that year. Every Thursday from 6:00-10:00 PM for the next year and a half, I sat in classroom again. When the NBA schedule was released, I was relieved to see that we only had one game on a Thursday night the entire season. We were only allowed one absence in each class, and I was thankful work wouldn't force me to miss class. However, I had not figured out childcare for my son.

I was already asking for help on game nights, and then needed help at least one additional night each week. Outside of the Thursday class sessions, we also had to meet with the study groups we selected on the first night of class for four hours each week. Because of the accelerate nature of the classes, the groups often met more often or for longer periods of time and extensive individual studying. I was considered a full-time student. I was also a full-time employee and a full-time mother.

Leaving work each Thursday at 5:00 PM with only enough time to grab a quick bite to eat at a fast food restaurant along the way and get to class by 6:00 PM, I called the designated babysitter for the day to ensure my son was situated before I entered the classroom. For the first few classes, I arranged for one of Jaylan's neighborhood friend's mother, Naomi, to pick him up from his afterschool program. She picked him up, and the boys did their homework together and some nights she would even make him take a bath before I arrived to pick him up. By the time I got to her house to pick him up about 10:30, I rushed to get him home and in the bed just as I had done when I began working for the Grizzlies.

Naomi was a very sweet lady who didn't mind helping me with Jaylan, but I never wanted to be a burden to anyone and didn't want to ask for her help too often or for too long. Because the classes were accelerated, they lasted only six weeks with the exception of two classes which were eight weeks long. When I moved from one class to the next, I found a new babysitter.

Another friend of mine named Staci, whom I met while pledging my sorority, joined my babysitter rotation program. Like Naomi, Staci made sure homework was done and that Jaylan was ready for bed by the time I picked him up after I got out of class. Hearing about the movies they watched and songs they liked, I smiled as Jaylan expressed how much fun he had with Staci. He liked all of my friends, and they all loved him.

When I moved to Memphis for college, I only knew my two high school friends who moved with me. However, God blessed me to meet so many more friends who supported me on my journey. I was so thankful to have them all in my life. Other than a couple of cousins who helped me occasionally, I did not have any family in town, and I relied primarily on the friends I made while in college and working at the Grizzlies to help me achieve my goals and take care of my son.

On nights when I didn't have a babysitter, Jaylan attended class with me like he had done in undergraduate school. Unlike when I was in undergraduate school where Jaylan practiced writing his letters and numbers while I was in class, by the time I was in graduate school, he was doing his homework when he attended class with me.

He really was a good child. Other than the fact that he was cute and people just wanted to play with him at times, he disturbed the class very little. I was thankful because I had to bring him to class with me at least one night of each class. He even came to our weekly group meetings.

Typically, my group of four ladies met in one of our homes or at a nearby bookstore. In the bookstore, Jaylan finished his homework, read children's books, or looked at books on cars while we worked. His presence never kept me from doing what I needed to do to create better lives for both of us, but I constantly fought guilt for not being with him as much as I wanted.

On Thursdays and most game nights, I kissed him goodbye in the morning before he headed to his bus stop down the street from our house, and I didn't see him again until after ten at night. In the evenings that I did not have class or have to work, I tried to make up time with him.

Hugging me before walking out the door, he inquired, "Do you have to work tonight, Ma?"

Happy that there was not a game that I night, I responded, "No, baby. I sure don't."

He continued his questioning with, "Do you have to go to school?"

"Nope. I'm picking you up just like I did yesterday and I will tomorrow too. Love you, sweetie. Have fun at school."

Laughing, he responded, "I'll try." As he walked out the door, I watched him wearing the backpack that my dad had given him when he returned from his service in Iraq. Written in Arabic letters across the backpack was the name that I had given my son who was growing up too fast.

Once my baby was out of my sight, I finished getting dressed and headed to work thankful that I would have the evening to spend with him. Although I picked him up myself at least three out of five nights during the week, I felt guilty about not doing it the other two. Back home in the evenings, I usually cooked something quick and allowed him to help. Then we did his homework which included everything from reading assignments and math worksheets to elaborate projects that were actually parent homework rather than assignments student could do independently. While completing the assignments that took anywhere from ten minutes to two hours to complete, I struggled to get insight about his day at school.

"What did you do at school today?" I inquired.

He responded, "Nothing," as he shrugged his shoulders. I couldn't believe he had already gotten to the stage where he didn't get excited about divulging every detail of the school day.

"Nothing? Well, what did you do in math?" He forced me to call out each subject in order to find out what happened that day. After enough questions, he warmed up and openly shared the extra information about school that day.

Once homework was out of the way, we had a little fun on some nights. Selecting a board game from the collection of junior version games he had gotten for Christmas, he usually beat me and sometimes without me letting him. We watched maybe an hour of television while we ate dinner and talked more before it was time to begin preparing for the next day. He had started selecting his own clothes so I would examine his planned outfit, make any adjustments, and help him iron his clothes. To save time, we developed the practice of selecting and ironing his clothes for the entire week on Sundays to save us time through the week. We also prepared lunches on Sundays when he no longer qualified for free lunch. Stuffed brown paper bags were lined up in the refrigerator so that he could quickly grab one on his way to the bus stop,

However, many days the bags contained nothing more than a sandwich and other days we made other arrangements. When I didn't have time or money for a trip to the grocery store, we had to improvise. Occasionally, when time was more of the issue than money, I would write a check for his lunch for the week. Grinning as I watched him grab the check on the counter, I was reminded of when Brandy and I snatched up our lunch money checks left by my stepfather and ran out the door to catch the bus. I didn't realize until I had to provide lunch for my own child how important my stepfather's simple gesture of writing a check was especially once I understood my parent's financial constraints. I was thankful that I had money in the bank to be able to write that check.

Occasionally, I brought lunch to him. When I got the request, "Ma, can you come and eat with me today?" I tried my best to accommodate. Leaving work downtown in time to make it to his favorite restaurant and to his school, I enjoyed a thirty-minute meal with my son as he proudly showed me off to his friends and not-so-discretely pointed to the girls he liked and the ones who liked him. He began to choose and iron clothes and prepare lunches with no help from me. He was growing up and getting more and more independent each day and each year.

During the summers, I sought full-time child care and the cost had to be as close to free as possible. Although he was uncomfortable with it at first, Jaylan eventually got used to the new kids he met each summer at the free community summer camps I found each year. When I began to make more money, I could afford to pay for basketball camps which he enjoyed. Whether he spent the day at a babysitter's house, a community or basketball camp, or occasionally at the office with me, I explained that I was doing what I had to do and that our situation was only temporary. One day we'd have more money, more time, and more family.

His bedtime was 8:30 PM, and that was both for him and for me. He was a young child and needed to go to bed at a reasonable time, and I needed time for myself. Occasionally, I made time for a phone conversation or quick peak at an interior design show or the news, but most of the time I only got to do my homework. In my classes, we moved through the coursework rapidly which meant I had a lot of reading to do on my own and the few hours after Jaylan was asleep was my key time to catch up.

Although busy at work, I found time to do homework there too. Lunch breaks proved to be an optimal time for reading and studying. I watched my work friends, Teresa and Staci, leave for lunch while I sat at my desk or in the break room working on a paper or reading an assignment. Teresa was my sorority sister and one of my best friends, and I enjoyed spending lunch time with her and Staci talking about the challenges and events of our lives from challenges at work to personal issues. I no longer had much spare time to talk; only time to do. Not a minute of my day could be wasted and lunch time was sixty minutes that I could use so that I could maybe get to bed before midnight.

Pursuing my MBA was difficult. In fact, I contemplated quitting many times because I was tired and the end of the program seemed so far away. Although I was determined to finish what I had started, I reconsidered quitting school again when my job presented me with my next opportunity.

Lesson Learned:

♥ **Don't waste time.** Everyone is guilty of procrastination to various degrees. I learned after coming to work exhausted from staying up all night doing homework that I needed to find a more efficient use of my time. Day and night and even in my spare time at work, I spent my time doing things that would improve my situation. I tried to make decisions that would not keep me in the same situation.

Another Step Up

For no one on earth—from east or west, or even from the wilderness—should raise a defiant fist. It is God alone who judges; he decides who will rise and who will fall.
-Psalm 75:6-7

As I sat in my cubicle typing up a promotion idea to deliver Philly cheese steaks from one of our sponsors to radio stations at lunchtime to promote the upcoming Grizzlies vs. 76'ers game, Marla approached my desk and asked me to come to her office. She was smiling so I wasn't nervous that she had bad news, but I wondered what she had to tell me. When I entered her office, the new vice president of event marketing sat in a chair across from Marla's desk. I greeted her and took the empty seat next to her.

"Summer, I know you have a lot going on with Jaylan and with school, but we wanted to let you know something we'd like to do if you're interested."

Anxious to hear her thought, I asked, "Okay. What is it?"

"Well, now that we're gearing up to open the new arena, we will need a lot of help to support all the shows that we're gonna bring," chuckling as she continued, "I'm not willing to give you up so we thought this would be a great opportunity to promote you. We'd like you to be the marketing and promotions manager for basketball and events. You would help us make sure we're making the best use of our time and money in promoting both sides of the operation. Well, what do you think?"

Completely caught off guard by the offer, I didn't know what to think and definitely didn't know what to say.

Part of the agreement for the NBA team to move to Memphis from Vancouver was for the city to build a new arena that met NBA standards. For the first few seasons, the team had played in the Pyramid arena, while the new arena was being built. On games days, the staff made the short drive from our office to the Pyramid which was not owned and operated by the team. Once the new arena was built, the team handled all operations, sales, marketing, ticketing, etc. for all events coming to the arena including concerts, ice shows, circuses, basketball and more. Although basketball operations were covered, the team now handled all aspects of the new arena and needed to hire many new employees to manage the events side of the operation.

When the vice president of event marketing was hired, she handled securing and marketing all events outside of basketball. Marla continued to manage marketing for the basketball team. Aware that many of their marketing and promotions efforts would overlap, they were looking for someone to bridge the event and basketball endeavors and find synergies and cost savings where possible. Who was better to do this than the person who had been handling marketing and promotions for the team for the past two years? Actually, I was sure there were a lot of people more qualified for the job. Hundreds of resumes from qualified sports professionals at other teams and entertainment companies flooded the Grizzlies office daily. Most of the applicants had more experience in arena marketing than I had, but I had two things on my side-God's favor and the fact that I was already an employee of the company who knew the market.

Sitting in Marla's office, I finally responded to the proposal, "That sounds great, but I have to be honest with you because I don't want anyone to be disappointed. I know that everyone is watching us and the expectations are tremendous for the new arena. I just don't know..."

Marla interrupted, "Summer, you really know more than you think and what's most important are the relationships you've done such a great job of developing. We'll figure out the rest together."

Relieved by Marla's confidence in me that was greater than my own, I accepted the promotion to marketing and promotions manager for the Memphis Grizzlies *and* the FedExForum arena.

I was excited about the promotion and the thought of making more money, but I was afraid of the new responsibilities it entailed and the additional time it would take away from

Jaylan. I now not only had to be at games, but I also had to be at all arena events. I was already stretched very thin working regular business hours plus games which were two or three nights a week and some weekends plus class one night a week and group meetings an additional night each week. With all of that, I still had to study and do my homework and help Jaylan with his too. In my new role, I handled events too. Events included everything from concerts that ran one night to ice shows and circuses with up to eight shows. Most events overlapped with basketball season too. I contemplated the challenge before me, *How in the world can I be a good mother while continually adding things to my plate that take time away from him? Should I have declined the promotion, but will I ever have an opportunity like this again?*

I certainly wanted to be a marketing manager. Never in my wildest dreams did I imagine that I could have achieved that title so fast especially with the NBA. I considered putting school on hold until I got adjusted to my new position. After all, the primary reason that I was in graduate school was so that I could get promoted. However, when I considered the more personal reason I had gone back to school, I didn't want to stop the momentum I had already built. I wanted the satisfaction of knowing I could do it. I thought, *No, I can't stop now, but I can't give up this once in a lifetime opportunity either. Lord, I'm going to do both, and I need your help to make sure Jaylan doesn't suffer because ultimately this is all for him too.*

When I accepted the position, I had lots of questions. I wanted to make sure I did my best to set myself and the company up for success. My first question was, "Is there any kind of training I can go through that might help me learn arena marketing?"

The event marketing vice president replied, "Actually there is. You and I will be going to Toronto next month."

Attending a huge, yearly arena marketing conference in Toronto, Canada, I learned about the various shows and got marketing ideas. I also met many of the promoters who would be bringing shows to our new stadium. For the first time as a full-time Grizzlies employee, I got to take a business trip. And for the first time in my life, I traveled outside of the United States. The team covered the cost for the entire trip and for my passport that I later used as often as possible. Traveling for the company, I began to feel like an important part of the marketing team. I had to make several requests for help before finding someone who could not only pick Jaylan up afterschool for me, but also keep him overnight for three nights and take him to school in the mornings. However, I eventually did and, in the future, always worked it out.

Knowing that my job would require me to be away from home frequently, I searched for ways to gain some time at home. My supervisor had been given a laptop when she was hired, and I thought that might be a good solution for me so that I could work from home and spend at least a few hours with my son when he got home from school.

On the flight back from Toronto I asked, "I know this might be a stretch, but I think it will help me be more productive and will help me with my work/life balance. Do you think it would be possible for me to get a laptop?"

With a look of disbelief that made me feel dumb for asking the question, the event marketing vice president said, "Are you serious? No, that won't be possible. I need you in the office."

Sitting in a window seat, I turned to focus on the clouds rather than the insensitive woman I had agreed to sacrifice time with my son for. *Okay, no laptop for me. What else can I do?*

I learned my lesson and positioned my next, much loftier request to Marla instead. I asked for help. For nearly two years, I had been the marketing coordinator for the growing marketing team, but as the marketing manager I asked for a marketing coordinator for myself. I got one, but not only that. I also asked for a full-time intern, and I got that too.

Just three years prior, I was begging for a job with the team trying to sell myself knowing that I had no real business experience especially in sports marketing. Sold. Not a year after that, I was trying to convince the director of marketing to take a chance on me and let me stay with the team in whatever capacity she saw fit. Convinced. After that, I just did my best and the promotions were offered to me. I worked hard and did not complain because I knew my hard work and sacrifice would pay off. A manager position was created just for me, and I even got to write the job descriptions for the marketing coordinator and intern that I interviewed and hired.

Although I still attended games and events, I no longer had to attend *all* games and events. God gave me backup. I had support, and all I had to do was ask for it. God worked it out for me to be in the position I was in and even gave me help. I had some support from my friends too, but often, when I had to work a game or an event my friends were not able to pick him up for me. Oftentimes, I just didn't want to bother anyone.

On those occasions, I made the drive from my downtown job to Jaylan's afterschool program when I got off work and headed straight back to my office. I was blessed to get an office when I was promoted to manager so when we got back, Jaylan and I closed the door to my office and he did his homework while I finished preparing for the event of the night. Once he finished it, I let him watch cartoons on the television in my office until we headed to the arena where I found co-workers to help serve as babysitters throughout the event.

Even though I had help with managing events, I was solely responsible for entertaining artists and escorting them on the local media tours to promote the incoming event. From WWE wrestlers, Harlem Globetrotters, clowns, ringmasters, and even an award-winning Olympic gymnastics coach, I chauffeured passengers in my car or limos rented for the occasion to radio and television stations and other promotional appearances. It was a great experience, but getting these guests to media outlets meant starting my day as early as 6:30 AM to pick up the entertainers from their hotels to make all the television and radio morning show appearances. Although I pressed the snooze button multiple times on those early mornings, getting up was not the problem.

The challenge was that I had an elementary school son whose school did not open until 7:00 AM. When I usually had to make it downtown by 6:30 AM to pick up an artist, I was left with no choice but to take my baby to school before the doors open. I hated to do it, but I had to get to work and I felt like he was safe outside of his school. Every time I had to leave my young child outside those school doors as I drove to work, sometimes before daybreak, I cried and prayed, *Lord please watch over my baby. Don't let anyone or anything harm him.* Knowing I would need help in the evenings and not wanting to wake anyone just because I had to be up, I took the occasional chance and trusted God to protect him.

"Okay, Jay," I kneeled down and looked up at my baby as we stood in front of the school doors, "Just sit here and read your book. A teacher will be here in a little bit to let you in the school. Okay?"

"Ma, I'm okay," he reassured me.

"Okay. Love you. See you later."

"Love you too."

Later usually meant after he was asleep. Afternoon and evening radio and appearances, as well as events, were a challenge too. When hosting these guests, my days started early in the morning and went late into the night. When big celebrities were in town for concerts, I had the awesome privilege of presenting them with personalized jerseys and hosting meet and greet events with fans. I also interacted with NBA players on a regular basis either having to escort them at events or get their autographs for promotional or charitable purposes. Although I was grateful for the opportunity to meet these famous people, I felt like I was sacrificing the most important person to me.

To keep me focused on my end goal, I reflected on what God had already done for me and prepared myself for what I knew He still could do in my life. I had survived my initiation as a marketing manager. I continued to thrive in school, and I maintained my most important job as a mother. When asked how I did it all, I sighed with a tired smile, "I really don't know. I guess I really don't think about it. I just do it."

Lessons Learned:

♥ **My best *was* good enough.** I was working hard. I was not making a lot of money, but I was making my own money and it was enough to take care of my son. However, even though I had money, I sometimes felt like I was not really taking care of him. I felt like providing *money* for my child was keeping me from providing *time* for my child? I often beat myself up, but I knew I was doing my best and I would be rewarded for it.

♥ **It's just temporary.** I knew that working long hours and begging for help with my son wouldn't last forever. I prayed and continued to improve myself to make my sacrifice pay off as quickly as possible. I continued to do my best on my job and at school so that one day I would have *one* job that would provide me with the time and money I needed to be a better mother.

The Child and the Career

For his anger lasts only a moment, but his favor lasts a lifetime! Weeping may last through the night, but joy comes with the morning. -Psalms 30:5

For the time being at least, my job wasn't going to change. Managing my job and my child was a tough balancing act, but I handled it. I loved my son, I loved my job, and I was thankful when the job presented incredible opportunities for my son. Although my career hadn't led me to wealth yet and often kept me from spending time with my son, it did provide some perks that my son otherwise wouldn't have enjoyed.

According to Jaylan, he was one of the coolest students at school because his mother worked for the Grizzlies. He was proud of me, and he made sure everyone knew where I worked. Although I knew I was barely supporting us, he made me feel like I brought home a million dollars every paycheck. In addition to the clout he got at school, Jaylan had the opportunity to attend several NBA games and other events sitting in premium seats that I definitely couldn't afford to buy.

Other invaluable opportunities came his way too. One year, the team decided to incorporate a miniature version of the mascot into the game experience. Jaylan was asked to play the role and was measured for a costume. He was so excited and even told classmates to watch out for him at the games. A few weeks later when we were expecting to see the finished costume, I was given some bad news to relay to my ecstatic child.

I started, "Jaylan, I know you're excited about being mini-Grizz, but you know you'll be able to do some other things, right?"

Looking confused by my statement turned question, he replied, "Yes, ma'am, but I'm going to still get to be mini-Grizz, right?"

"Well, baby. When they thought about it again, they figured it would be easier if they had one of the kids on kid's dance team since they already know some of the routines big Grizz does."

Hurt and disappointed, he just murmured, "Okay."

"It'll be okay, Jaylan."

"Yes, ma'am," was his final response.

Although it made perfect sense to use a dancer, it did not make it any easier for me to have to tell Jaylan he was not going to get to do it. Everyone involved felt bad about it and wanted to make it up to him. I couldn't have asked for a better remedy than what was offered.

Not long after the disappointment of finding out some other child would be in the mini-Grizz costume, Jaylan was preparing to celebrate his ninth birthday. Like always, I wanted his birthday to be a fun, unique experience that he would always remember, but I didn't have the money to have a party for him. Then I got a visit from the marketing director, the mascot, and the director over the honorary ball boy program. In lieu of being mini-Grizz and hiding behind a costume for a few games each season, Jaylan was presented the opportunity to be an honorary ball boy. Another child who had won the position for the night was unable to attend and they needed someone else to do the job.

Jaylan manned a post on an actual NBA floor directly in front of the team for the entire game. Grabbing towels and catching breakaway pants thrown to him as players entered the game, he handled it like a professional. Instead of watching the game, I watched Jaylan on the sidelines from my seat in the stands nearly the entire game. I was so proud of him and so happy that, through my job that took so much time away from him, I was able to provide him with a once in a lifetime opportunity that my money could not have bought. At the end of the game, he entered the locker room with players and got autographs and took pictures with the team. Nearly able to count all the teeth in his mouth with a smile that never left his face, I listened to my baby talk about his night as I drove home that night. All the long nights and time away from him working for the team were worth it for that moment.

The following year for his tenth birthday, I knew that I couldn't top the opportunity he received for his ninth birthday and didn't even try. Instead, I planned a small party at the house with a few of his friends and some family with the familiar birthday party menu of hot dogs, chips, birthday cake and ice cream. I had gotten a promotion and a raise but not enough to change my standard of living so we still lived modestly. Although I knew he was fine with our unpretentious arrangements because he had learned to appreciate the little things, I was disappointed that I could not do more for him. With my salary increase, I had started saving money for his college education in an aggressive manner just like when I saved to buy my house.

At work the day before his birthday, I headed downstairs to go to the bank across the street from our office. As I began to cross the street, our vice president's secretary stopped me and asked me if I could use twelve tickets in the luxury suite for the Monster Trucks show the next night. She had no idea the next day was Jaylan's birthday; she only knew that none of the executives were interested or able to attend the show and that the suite would otherwise be empty. I had spent the past few weeks promoting the show, but Jaylan had never been to a Monster Trucks show. Neither had his friends so I figured it would be a fun, new experience for them. Instead of repeating the events from his fifth birthday party for his tenth, Jaylan spent his birthday with his friends watching a fascinating show that was perfect for boys and viewed it from a luxury suite. They loved it, and I was thankful I was able to give Jaylan another great birthday present I could not have bought with my own money.

As the team geared up for a new basketball season, Jaylan got an even greater benefit from my job. Because the director of marketing had always thought Jaylan was a cute and well-mannered child, when the team needed a model to promote our new giveaway series she called on my baby. That season, fans received various items including sports bags, jerseys, shorts, caps, basketballs and wristband and headband set over several games. As the model, Jaylan had a photo shoot that occurred the same night as another event. I found Jaylan in the arena sitting with my friend who had brought him, and I led him to the empty room where the photographer was set up. I answered my walkie-talkie as questions were asked and requests were made regarding the show that was taking place. I didn't want to rush my baby's moment, but I had to get back to work.

"Alright, let's put the bag across your shoulder and you can just hold the basketball," the photographer instructed as he finished positioning Jaylan for the shots.

"Yes, sir," Jaylan nervously replied trying to make sure he did everything just right, but he was happy and feeling very important.

After what seemed like a hundred photos, the photo shoot was done, and I returned Jaylan to my friend. When basketball season started, Jaylan's photograph became the symbol for the giveaway series and was featured in 10,000 game programs each game for 41 games during the regular season, in print ads that ran throughout the entire season, and on the team and arena Web sites. My baby's face was everywhere.

After seeing the print ads, the broadcast department decided to produce a television commercial to promote the giveaway series as well, and they wanted the same "talent" that was used for print promotion. Although he wasn't getting paid money for the role, I liked hearing him called talent as if he were a paid model or actor. Standing in the corridor of the new arena dressed in the items from the giveaway series, the little model turned actor followed the instructions of the camera man.

When they were finished, he ran up to me and gave me the biggest hug I had gotten in a long time, "Ma, that was so much fun! Thank you. I love you!"

"Baby, you did a great job! I'm so proud of you."

Although it really wasn't me, I thought to myself, *I'm so glad I was able to do something else for him. These days have been so long and so hard. He probably doesn't even remember how I look!*

The commercial was produced and played in-arena at every home game and in all game broadcasts which aired in three states. My parents watched the games regularly, and I wanted them to be surprised when they saw Jaylan's commercial so I didn't even let them know he had a commercial. Like many other people who recognized his face, they were shocked to see him on television. In the arena when the commercial played on the huge, four-sided screen that was suspended above everyone's head and when Jaylan was sitting in the stands, the fans around his seat would ask for his autograph. Modestly grinning as he signed his name in the cursive letters he had not too long before learned to write, he felt like he was an actual NBA player himself. Because I was able to see my job serving as an avenue to provide my son with opportunities he otherwise never would have seen, some of my guilt about time spent focusing on my career and educational development and away from my son was alleviated.

Since he was born, I wanted to give him more of my time. Fighting to be different than so many other single mothers I knew, I spent much of my time pursuing my education and working so that I could provide for my child in the future. I hated to always tell my son, "I'm sorry, I can't afford that," any time he asked for things as simple as clothes or a toy. Still unable to buy what I just couldn't afford, I sought opportunities like those provided by the Grizzlies. I did all I could to provide a good childhood for him. I wanted him to be happy despite the fact that he would never know his father or possibly any father and might never have another child in the house to develop with him. From the time he started school, I heard his words-both spoken and unspoken-of pain and confusion from not having that in his life.

I was thankful that God had blessed me with Jaylan and that he was such a good child, but he was still a child. At times he challenged me by talking back, by not cleaning his room and in all the other ways children do their parents. Not doing his best at school and bringing home bad grades at times, he was like most normal children and needed punishment and discipline as well as rewards and exciting opportunities. Providing that discipline for someone who desperately needed it but who just as desperately needed extra love and understanding tested me as a single mother. I was always compelled to find something to give my son to compensate for what I couldn't give him and tried to create a healthy balance between rewards and punishments.

How do I punish someone I feel so sorry for? It's not his fault he doesn't have a daddy and probably feels he barely has a mother. His grandparents aren't here with him, and he is always being shuffled around. Is he just acting out, crying for attention?

Clear matters of right and wrong like disobeying a rule or saying inappropriate words were easy to punish; however, I had difficulty diagnosing and punishing him for other actions like the declining grades which I sometimes saw as a symptom rather than the actual problem.

An additional challenge with discipline was that punishing him often meant punishing myself. Letting him stay with friends and even having his friends over meant breaks for me and opportunities to do things I normally couldn't. When he was confined, so was I.

Without family in town, I was short on options for sitters beyond my friends who wanted to go out and his own friend's parents which would mean fun for Jaylan. Even as a teenage mother, I had been firm with my child. In fact, my friends often begged me to show more mercy in dealing with my son. However, I insisted on enforcing punishment. Because I knew one day he would grow up and be bigger and stronger than me, I demanded his respect at an early age.

I longed for my son to have a father to guide him into manhood and help discipline him with love, as well as brothers and sisters so that he wouldn't grow up alone. I had a child who regularly expressed wanting a daddy, but no relationships up to that pointed had lasted. I hesitated to even try out of fear of getting hurt myself, and more importantly, hurting my son.

Growing up, I imagined having a traditional household where the father primarily provided the discipline with a good balance of fear and respect while the mother was gentler and provided love and got respect as well. Not that either of the households I lived in fell in the traditional mold, but I still wanted that for my family. I quickly learned that the majority of households don't operate like that sometimes even when both parents are in the home. Like those families I had to find another solution for raising my son. Using the model in my mind, I played the tough, "I was a boy before so I know what he's up to" dad who taught my son about his body and how to treat girls. However, I also served in my natural role as his sweet, loving mother always wanting to believe the best of my son. All he had was me, but he needed both.

My son was probably just as confused as I was as I tried to surmount that challenge daily. Juggling my time between motherhood, school and work and managing my tiny bank account was a difficult task; however, it was nothing compared to being a mother and a father in one body. I had to be tough on him because I was raising a man and at the same time I had to ensure he felt loved by the only parent he had.

Looking for opportunities to expose my son to new experiences and reward him for good behavior, I booked a flight one winter to Washington, D.C. to visit Chinitra who had been living there since we graduated from college. I had visited her before, but that trip I decided to take Jaylan on his first flight. As a child, I never had the opportunity to travel much further than to Bolivar or Nashville to visit my father. Flying was not even a consideration. In all aspects of my life, I wanted to give my son opportunities and expose him to positive experiences I never had or didn't have at his age. I prepared for the trip months in advance by saving to buy our airline tickets. Staying at Chinitra's house, we only needed money for our flights.

"Are you scared, baby?" I inquired of my grade school-aged child.

"Um, not really," he responded with a confident smile that convinced me that he wasn't worried at all.

"You wanna sit by the window or not?"

"I kinda do, but you can if you want to," he responded. I loved when he was in his extra courteous moods.

"It's all yours sweetie," I insisted motioning for him to move over to the window.

As Jaylan sat staring at and marveling over the clouds, I remembered that wasn't actually his first flight. In fact, he had even been to Washington, D.C. Not even ten years earlier, I was sitting like him staring out at the clouds too. Instead of asking questions about the clouds and the plane like he did, I sat quietly with my thoughts about the thing growing inside of me. On my first flight, I was preparing for an abortion when I returned home rather than focusing on the adventure of the trip. I was thankful that his trip to DC was nothing like mine and that he got to enjoy the innocence of his childhood on his first plane ride.

When we landed, Chinitra greeted us as we claimed our luggage. We stopped at a fast food restaurant and headed to her place to rest before getting back out to Dave and Buster's later that night. Our big exploration occurred the following day.

Although snow covered the ground, Jaylan and I explored the National Mall the next day while Chinitra attended meetings that she couldn't reschedule. Starting on one end on the right side of the long, narrow Reflecting Pool in the center of the mall, we made our brisk stroll that cold, winter day visiting the historic sites of the Lincoln Memorial, the Washington Monument, and the Vietnam Veterans Memorial. Although Jaylan didn't know a lot about the tributes to historical figures and events, he had at least heard of them in class. On our tour, he especially enjoyed the Smithsonian museums where we rushed in escaping the cold. From the National Air and Space Museum and the National Museum of Natural History to the National Museum of the American Indian and the American History Museum, we spent an entire day absorbing all the images and knowledge presented to us. Like his exploits with the Grizzlies, he remembered the details of it long after it was over.

Lessons Learned:

♥ **Sometimes when opportunities are taken away it is because God has something better for us.** Jaylan was devastated when he didn't get to be the mini-mascot. However, had he been given that opportunity, he never would have gotten the chance to be a ball boy which he enjoyed much more than he would have enjoyed being in a costume all game.

♥ **Find the positive in the negative.** Sometimes the positive aspects of a situation are right in our faces, but other times we have to look for them. My time-consuming job took a lot away from my son, but it also gave a lot back to him.

♥ **Move, travel, and see the world.** When I moved away from Jackson and especially when I began to travel to different cities, I realized that seeing new places and meeting different types of people broadened my mind and exposed me to the vast possibilities available to me.

♥ **Expose children to new experiences.** After Jaylan's first time flying, he wanted to go everywhere. After seeing the sites at the museums, he wanted to go other places and learn more. Remove the limits on their minds and show them they can do anything and go anywhere.

Beyond Just the Two Us

"For where two or three gather together as my follower, I am there among them."- Matthew 20

Since I was fifteen, my entire life was devoted to being a mother, finishing and starting school, and working. I tried to make time for fun and enjoyed being with my friends and being a normal teenager and college student as best as I could, but everything revolved around and usually involved my son. Unlike my friends who all had boyfriends, I almost always didn't. Of course I wanted to be in relationships and actually did at times, but even when I was, I could not be like my friends and enjoy going on dates with my boyfriend or even spend a lot of time on the phone talking to him. Although I wanted them, relationships with guys were few and far between.

Several obstacles made having a boyfriend hard for me. First of all, when I gave birth to Jaylan I was only fifteen and had not been given permission to "date" yet. There had been a few boys I claimed as my boyfriend in the past, but that didn't mean anything because we were so young and didn't even see each other outside of school. Another reason was because even as I got older, I was still somewhat shy and uncomfortable around boys because of my acne problem and body perception. Finally, the primary reason I didn't have a relationship was because from the day I had Jaylan and went back to school, I was busy. Building a better life for my son and me was my main priority, and I just fit relationships in if, when and how I could.

In my ninth grade year of high school, I had my first real boyfriend, Markus. However, after finding out Jaylan was not his baby, Markus moved on and dated other people. And, once I had Jaylan, everything changed. I longed to be a normal teenage girl free of the responsibility of caring for a baby while struggling to finish high school.

How can I add a boyfriend to my already overflowing plate? I'm only in high school, but I'll be taking care of Jaylan, going to college and working a job for at least five more years. Am

I supposed to wait 'til after that to have a boyfriend? This ain't fair!

It wasn't fair, but it was my life. I decided that if having a boyfriend was something I wanted, then I could add it to the plate even if it was sitting on top of something else. In my senior year of high school, I accepted the request of a boy named Eric who had graduated two years earlier and became his girlfriend. Incorporating Eric into my life, I introduced him to my toddler so that I wouldn't have to take away time from Jaylan to be with Eric. Eric was nice and fun and enjoyed spending time with Jaylan and me. Whether we were sitting at Eric's parents' house or my grandmother's house or going out to eat or to a basketball game, almost everything we did involved Jaylan. The fact that I was a mother never seemed to bother Eric. However, like most relationships, our relationship as boyfriend and girlfriend soon ended.

Although breakups in relationships were normal, they were more difficult for me and posed much greater implications for my son. When Jaylan said, "Ma, what happened to Eric and...Jonathan...Anthony...and...Brian...and...?" I knew I had messed up by letting him meet different guys. His list seemed to go on and on with him even naming guys that were just my friends. I thought, *But I was just trying to make sure I didn't neglect my son just to be with my boyfriend. I had to combine them. How can I have time to have a boyfriend if he can't be around my child? What am I supposed to do?*

Initially, my trepidation around dating with a child was finding someone who would accept me and my child. On the surface, that didn't seem to be an issue as none of the guys I dated expressed any concerns about me having a child. Maybe my child wasn't a serious factor because we were still so young and they weren't thinking long-term about the relationship with me. Remembering my son's question, my apprehension turned from fear of acceptance as a mother to fear of the affect on my son when the relationship was over. Although I loved hard and hurt deeply, I was even less concerned about my own feelings when a relationship ended. I had a son who desperately wanted a father, and the last thing I wanted to do was make him think he had one just for that man to leave our lives.

I didn't want Jaylan to meet anyone else. I decided going into college that I had to take greater caution before introducing new men to my son and would only let Jaylan meet guys that I felt would be more than just my boyfriend and had serious potential of being the husband I wanted and the daddy he needed. I could no longer combine my time with them. One of the boys would get less of my time, and it could not be my son who was already getting too little of it.

How can I tell when someone will become more than just a boyfriend and when it's time to meet my son? How will I even have the time to date someone enough to get to know them? I don't have much free time, and I want to spend that with my son and with my boyfriend if I have one. I don't even have time to talk on the phone because I feel guilty leaving Jaylan alone while I talk on the phone, and I'm definitely not talking to anyone around his sponge ears that soak up everything. After he goes to bed, I have to do my homework. How do I finagle this? Am I not supposed to be with anyone?

In college, I dated a couple of guys but avoided letting Jaylan know I was in a relationship with any of them. They only saw Jaylan in group settings like on campus at step shows, meetings or other school functions that Jaylan attended with me, but they never got introduced to him any differently than my female friends. In my senior year of college, I finally introduced someone to Jaylan as my boyfriend.

A player on the school basketball team, Jason was the first man I felt I was in love with since high school and I was sure we would stay together. Either at his campus apartment that he shared with three of his teammates or at my apartment that I shared with Chinitra, Jason spent a lot of time with Jaylan and me. With Jason, I imagined myself with the complete family I always wanted.

Although he was a nice guy, he was a young, attractive athlete and didn't resist the temptation of all the girls vying for his attention. Three months after Jaylan and I both fell in love with him, Jason cheated and our relationship ended. For months after our breakup, Jaylan asked, "Ma, why can't we go to Jason's house today? I want to play the game with him." I thought, *Great. More tough questions for me. Why do I always have to answer the hard questions and do the hard things when I wasn't the one who did something wrong? He cheated on me! He should have to tell Jaylan why he's no longer in our lives.*

Because Jaylan had always been a very mature child, I felt like I could be upfront and open with him. As a small child, I explained how he was conceived and why he didn't have a father so why not be honest with him about why he couldn't be around Jason anymore. I explained that, "Well, Jaylan. I know we had fun playing video games with Jason and watching basketball games with him. He's a nice person, and still cares about you. You know he was my boyfriend, but then he wanted to have two girlfriends. Remember how I told you that you can just have one?" He looked confused but still nodded. I continued, "When you have more than one, you lose the best one. Now he's not my boyfriend so we can't go over his house anymore. We'll just play video games here or over your friend's house." Crying alone in my room, I was hurt because I loved Jason but was more embarrassed to face my son and devastated to have to explain that to him. Another man in and out. Another man on Jaylan's mental list of mama's boyfriends and still no daddy.

Although Jason was out, his younger cousin, Alexis was in. She was a high school student and an only child who desired an older sister. I became that to her and she became my occasional babysitter, my friend, and my mentee. With this new relationship, she always invited Jaylan and me to attend church with her since we did not have a church home in Memphis. Jason and his whole family attended the church so we saw him when we were there. After church, we were invited to Jason's grandparent's house for Sunday dinner. Like in a scene from the movie *Soul Food,* his entire family was together enjoying lots of good, home-cooked food and the company of family. I sat around the dining room table talking with the women while the men watched TV in the living room and the children, including the biggest child, Jason, played video games in the back. Because I didn't really have family in Memphis, Jaylan and I always accepted the invitation and enjoyed the company nearly every Sunday for almost three years.

Although they were not actually my family, I was treated as they were and they insisted that Jaylan and I continue to come over even when Jason had new girlfriends who were at the house too. At times it was a bit awkward seeing my old boyfriend that I still had feelings for with someone else, but the family always showed that it didn't matter and made me feel like a family member rather than Jason's ex-girlfriend. I enjoyed the feeling of family so much that we continued attending church and eating Sunday dinner with them until I started a new relationship and found a new church to call my own.

One year at a party on Thanksgiving night, I was approached by a guy named Michael and we hit it off immediately. After hosting my family at my new house for Thanksgiving, I let Jaylan go to Jackson with my mother for the weekend and I spent the time with my new friend. I had finally met someone I liked as much as I had cared for my past boyfriends, and I was happy.

When Jaylan got back to town a few days later, I was ready for him to meet my new friend because I knew we'd all be spending a lot of time together. Michael came over and played games with Jaylan. Bending a wire hanger to form a basketball rim and securing it at the top of a door, Michael shot socks, paper wads, and whatever else that would fit through the makeshift rim with Jaylan. Jaylan loved it. And I loved seeing him get that attention from a man, the father figure that he had been craving since he started school and realized other children had daddies. The relationship with my new boyfriend was great when it was good and horrible when it was bad, and after a few months it was over.

Although it seemed like it would last forever, it did not. Michael cheated on me, and I ended our relationship. Normally, I parked my car on the far left side of my garage so that when Michael visited, he could fit his truck in my garage. After a few days of me parking my car in the middle of the garage, Jaylan asked, "Ma, why are you parking like this? Is Michael not coming back?" Embarrassed and hurting myself and for Jaylan, I thought,

I've done it again. Another one out the door and on the list. I felt like I basically kept telling my son, "Jaylan, here's that father you've always wanted." I just always seemed to leave out the part that he would not be with us very long.

This time the explanation to Jaylan was a little easier. Looking at the boy I was grooming to be a man, I simply said, "Jaylan, do you remember why I told you Jason wasn't my friend anymore?" Jaylan just nodded his head. In that moment, I thought about the reason that I had determined that God had given me a son when all along I was expecting a daughter. God wanted me to raise a God-fearing man who would love, honor and respect women and eventually be a good husband and a good father. I prayed that my son's exposure to my boyfriends who were not good examples would have an inverse effect and make him a better man.

However, while I was with Michael, he introduced me to his church, New Direction Christian Church. The church was new and had a young, dynamic pastor and a fast-growing congregation. Even after our breakup, I continued to attend the church with my son, and we eventually joined. I felt that one of God's reasons for allowing Michael to come into my life was to introduce me to this church where Jaylan and I were growing in our walk with Christ. After only a few months as members, my young son asked me, "What do I have to do to get baptized?" I couldn't have been prouder when, a few weeks later, I watched with my mother, grandmother and a couple of friends as my baby professed his belief in Jesus Christ and was put under the water and came up as a new little "man". He told me he was ready. I didn't even have to ask him. Remembering what my pastor told me when I got baptized, "Now you really have to watch out because Satan is upset with you. He's gonna come after you hard," I watched and prayed over and with my baby daily.

My baby was definitely growing up. He was starting to understand spirituality, life and families. Like when he was at school, he witnessed fathers and sons with other siblings sitting together and interacting at church. Although he had stopped requesting it as much as he used to, he wanted a father and even expressed wanting a little brother. "Ma, do you think you'll ever get married?"

"Well, I'd like to, but I have to wait on God to bless me with the right person to be my husband," I replied knowing that I'd been praying for a good husband to help me raise my son since he was born.

Pausing to think for a moment, he posed the next question, "Will you have another baby then? I want a brother."

Releasing a small laugh to keep tears from forming, I replied, "Well, I'd like that too, but it's very hard having a baby without a husband. You and me have been doing pretty good, but you know how I always have to find somebody to keep you when I have to work and I always say I can't afford stuff? It would be even harder with a baby in the house. Plus, God wants us to be married before we have babies so all kids can have a mother and a father. Once I get married I'll have more kids. Okay?" Knowing my own circumstances and another single parent child that Jaylan knew, I continued with, "But sometimes we don't do things like God wants us to or other things happen and we have to do the best we can with our situations but we can't continue to do wrong when we know better." And that's what we were doing-making the best of our situation. Looking in his sad eyes, I saw my answers weren't good enough. He needed more. He still wanted a daddy. As I often did, I held back my tears with a smile and softly said, "Baby, I love you enough for a hundred daddies anyway."

No matter how much I loved Jaylan, I knew I just could not be a daddy. I taught him about our Heavenly Father and took him to church regularly to help him develop that relationship, but I was praying for an earthly father for Jaylan too. I was clearly a woman and had no idea how to be a man or how to teach my son to be one. Other than what I knew I liked and did not like in men, I just did not know how to raise a man.

As Jaylan grew, my desire to have a husband for me and a father for him grew too. When I gave birth to Jaylan, I immediately loved my baby even though I thought I couldn't because of how he was conceived. Although there were times in my depression when I did not like him or even myself, I did love my baby. However, I also wondered what it would be like to have a baby with someone I knew and loved, who loved me, who loved *our* child, and who would help me raise the child to his or her greatest potential. I wondered all my life what it would be like to have someone to do it and go through the joys and challenges of being a parent with me.

I wondered, *How would it feel to have some help? How different would my life be? More importantly, how much better would his life be?* It had to be better than what I had experienced my whole life doing it alone. Yes, I was blessed to have support when I asked for it, but I never had relief. No one ever freely offered to take my son off my hands from time to time to give me a break or time to myself. No one visited or volunteered to just spend some time with him. I was always asking for help or struggling doing everything alone.

Looking up, I cried out questioning God, "Why am I still alone?" I continued my conversation internally with God,

Lord, what's wrong with me? I'm a good person. I'm responsible, caring and loving. I have a good job. I take care of my child. Why can't any of my relationships last? Why do I have to keep explaining to my son why the men who he thought might be a daddy to him keep leaving? I'm tired of saying, 'But I am here and I'm not going anywhere!' and putting on a fake smile to keep back my tears and pretending to be so strong for my baby.

Not willing to deal with the disappointment and not wanting to give the same explanation to Jaylan that he'd heard too many times before, I didn't get involved with anyone for the next two years. I refused to allow anyone else to enter our lives just to hurt and disappoint us when they left.

One day on the radio while Jaylan and I were riding home in the little green Sunfire, Will Smith's song that he re-made with his son, *"Just the Two of Us"* started playing. As the song played, Jaylan joined in pointing at me and back at himself as he bobbed his head. I smiled and started singing it back to him while I bobbed my head to the beat too. I had mixed feelings though. We were laughing and singing, but I didn't want it to be just the two of us. Neither did he. I loved my baby so much, but I wanted him to have more than just me. He needed a daddy too.

Lessons Learned:

♥ **There's a purpose in every relationship.** Meeting my ex-boyfriend Jason provided me with a sense of family in a city where I didn't have family. Although the relationship with him did not last, I gained a babysitter and was able to impact his cousin's life. Meeting Michael led me to my church home where my son made the decision for himself to be baptized. Be thankful from the good in every situation, and learn from the bad.

♥ **No more children until marriage.** Struggling as a teen mother, I knew I had to be able to give a child the support they need-time, financial, and emotional. So many teenage mothers have one child, then another and another until going to school or having a job seems impossible and there is only time to be a mother. Yet, in those cases they are a mother and they are not able to provide for their children themselves because oftentimes they are dependent on public assistance. However, even for the young, single mother of multiple children, life is not over.

Yet Another Finish Line

And all nations will hate you because you are my followers. But everyone who endures to the end will be saved.
-Matthew 10:22

Instead of dwelling on the fact that my relationships were always ending rather than growing, I concentrated on my own development and focused on finishing graduate school. Times did get hard, but I persevered. I kept a smile on my face when inside I was suppressing tears that I would release only when I was alone in my car or once my son was asleep. Maintaining a strong front, I spoke positively although many times I felt like giving up. Despite so many challenges, I finally earned my MBA and celebrated what, to me, was my biggest accomplishment yet.

To the party themed "Dreams Do Come True", I invited my closest friends and family. Standing before the crowd with Jaylan by side, I attempted a thank you speech. However, my tears overpowered my words, and I struggled to even get out, "Thank you all for coming."

Not long after my MBA celebration party, I stood in the church parking lot talking to a friend one night after Bible study. As Jaylan sat in the car finishing his homework while my friend and I talked, a guy with long dreadlocks named Everett approached us with a flyer promoting his candle-making business. Frowning because he had interrupted our conversation, I looked at his flyer then we continued our conversation as he drove off.

Two weeks later as Jaylan and I walked through a mall near our house, the guy with the dreadlocks approached me again. Standing outside of the barbershop where he worked, he offered Jaylan a free haircut and me a free eyebrow arch. I declined twice as we walked past the shop to other stores, but he was persistent. Finally, I thought to myself, *I might as well let Jaylan get a free haircut. I hate going to barbershops and at least I can let him go in there and get his haircut while I walk around the mall.* After he finished, Jaylan rushed over to me excitedly asking as he rubbed his head, "Can he be my new barber? This haircut is fresh!" I agreed. After all, Everett said the haircuts would be free.

After Jaylan's first haircut, Everett asked me to dinner. Dinner had always been off limits because the evenings and the weekends were my time for Jaylan. Lunch was the only option, but I was not interested in having lunch with him. However after a few haircuts and eyebrow arches, I finally accepted his offer.

When he picked me up from my office downtown, half a dozen red roses greeted me as I opened the passenger side door of his nice car. Driving just a couple of blocks away from my office, we dined at a swanky restaurant in an upscale hotel. Although he appeared shy and uncomfortable, we had good conversation. He was such a sweet guy and I could tell that he really liked me.

When I returned to the office with my half dozen roses in hand, a co-worker sarcastically remarked, "All he gave you was a *half* dozen."

"I don't care how many it is. Do you know the last time I had a single flower from anybody? Me either." I continued, "I love my roses," as I placed the vase on my desk near the window of my office. As I sat in my office admiring the roses my new friend had given me, my phone rang and the receptionist informed me that I had a delivery. My co-worker who had joked about my half dozen roses offered to pick up my delivery from the receptionist. My mouth dropped when he walked back into my office with a *full* dozen red roses with a note that simply read, "Dinner?" Although he was a nice guy who had just made my day, I still was not ready to give up my evening from Jaylan and find a babysitter just for me to go on a date. Everett would just have to continue being our barber friend.

My lunch date with Everett remained a secret from Jaylan because I refused to get his hopes up thinking that I had a new boyfriend. When Everett asked, "Can I hang out with you and Jaylan sometimes?" I immediately responded, "No! I mean, that's sweet of you, but we can't do that. We've been through too much, and I can't let him down again."

"Summer, I promise I'm not going anywhere. He's a good kid, and I just want to be able to spend some time with him and you too."

"I'm sorry, but I can't do that. You just don't understand how hurt he'll be when you decide to leave us alone."

"I'm not. Please give me a chance. Okay, how about you let me be like a big brother to him? You said you were going to try to get him a big brother at the church. Well, why don't you let me?"

Two years before meeting Everett, I placed Jaylan on the long waiting list at the Big Brothers, Big Sisters office. The list was full of little black boys in single mother homes with mothers like me, desperately seeking a male role model for their sons. Once Jaylan was assigned a "Big" as they call the mentors, the relationship only lasted a few months. His Big was also a father of three boys and realized that he just did not have the time to devote to my son. However, while he was Jaylan's Big, he signed him up for football and Jaylan got to experience being on a team which he enjoyed. When his Big stopped calling, Jaylan expressed the same disappointment as when my relationships ended. It seemed like men were always in and right back out of our lives and no man was consistently there for my son.

Although I often politely asked for help, many times I cried out for it. Sometimes I would get a temporary response with a cousin coming and spending a few hours or even an entire day with him only to disappear until my next cry for help. I begged for a consistent male presence in his life, but I could never achieve it. Since participating in the big brother program and wanting a father his entire life, Jaylan obviously missed that interaction with a man and I desperately wanted him to have it again. However, protecting my son was even more important than protecting my own heart. I believed Everett genuinely cared about Jaylan. Finally, I gave Everett an answer, "Okay, but please don't hurt him. Please don't disappoint me."

Why does everything have to be so complicated for me? I can't even just date to get to know people without worrying about hurting Jaylan. This really isn't fair. I just want to be normal.

Everett, please don't hurt my baby. I pray I'm doing the right thing by letting you in.

At the barbershop after Everett finished cutting Jaylan's hair, he told me to stay at the shop while he ran to a store in the mall with Jaylan. Returning with a bag containing a shoebox, Jaylan said, "Look what Everett got me!" as he handed me the bag. Smiling at Everett with disbelief and even slight disapproval, I said, "Oh, he shouldn't have done that, but that was nice. Tell him thank you."

"I did already, Ma."

"Okay, did Everett tell you he wants to be your new big brother?"

"Yes, ma'am. He said we were going to go to the arcade and go bowling and whatever else I wanted to do."

"That's nice, baby. We'll see."

I smiled at Everett, and he smiled back. I think his smile meant he was happy and proud to have made Jaylan so happy, but my face only shielded the fear in my heart. *Everett, please don't let my baby down.*

As Jaylan's new big brother, Everett spent time with Jaylan both with and without me. Joking and laughing all evening as we bowled more gutter balls than strikes, we all had fun on the bowling date Everett had been requesting for weeks. I enjoyed watching Everett instructing Jaylan and even teasing him. As Jaylan continued to get comfortable with Everett, I allowed Everett to pick him up some days after school and on the weekends so that Jaylan could help out at the barbershop and earn some money. Sweeping hair and cleaning mirrors, Jaylan enjoyed the time he spent with Everett, and I was thankful to have him in our lives. I observed as Everett showed Jaylan how to hold the bowling ball, and he eventually showed Jaylan how to hold a pool stick and even a mop.

When I signed Jaylan up for the church basketball team, Everett often went with us to his practices and even assisted the coach during games. Although, there was still no love connection, Everett was quickly becoming a great friend to me and to my son.

Everett acted like a natural father because he was one.

When Jaylan opened our front door to let Everett in, his mini-me stumbled in before him. His two-year-old son, Alan, shyly waved then clung to his daddy's leg. Always good with little children probably because he desperately wanted a sibling of his own, Jaylan reached for Alan's hand and asked, "Do you want to play with some toys in my room?"

Looking up for approval from his dad, Alan walked away with Jaylan. That was the first of many nights that Everett and I spent with both of our boys.

It was no secret that Everett wanted to be more than my friend. Through daily emails he revealed his feelings and made me feel more desired than I'd ever felt in my life. He told me I was beautiful and even thanked me for forcing us to remain just friends for so long. I began to fall for him, but I still was not sure I wanted to be more than friends to him. With my poor history with relationships, I didn't want to take a chance on letting another man into our lives in that capacity. I didn't trust men and was tired of being hurt and disappointing my son. I wondered, *Is this different? We've been friends longer than anyone else I've dated and Jaylan knows him now. Should I take another chance?*

I knew Everett was a Lyfe Jennings fan so when I got the opportunity to meet the artist I immediately thought about my relationship with Everett. In town to perform a concert, Lyfe Jennings inquired about taking a tour of Staxx Museum and he also wanted a personalized Grizzlies jersey. Part of my job at the Grizzlies was handling personalized jerseys for celebrities, and I got to fulfill that request. Almost ready to commit to Everett and give a new relationship a try, I told myself, *If Lyfe's promoter offers me tickets to the concert tonight, then I'll take Everett and give him his wish. He's really proven that he cares about me and Jaylan. I feel like we're safe with him.* Still fearful of relationships, I gave myself an out by saying to myself that if the promoter didn't give me tickets then I wouldn't start a new relationship with Everett.

I was given four tickets to the show and immediately called Everett to tell him that we were going. At the show, we sang, danced, and laughed, and I had the best time I had experienced in a long time. I waited all night to let Everett know that I would be his girlfriend still afraid to make our relationship official. Although I was only committing to be his girlfriend, I felt like I was accepting a marriage proposal.

I thought, *Okay, Summer. Once you do this, there's no turning back. Are you absolutely sure?*
Sitting in his car about to leave the concert, I finally did it. "Everett, I have something to tell you," I started.

Removing his hand from the steering wheel, he turned and looked at me and said, "What's up?"

"Um, I've been thinking about everything you said and everything you've done these last few months. You know I'm scared to be in a relationship again, but I decided I want to try. If you'll still have me, yes, I'll be your girl."

Initially, he didn't say a word. He only stared at me. Then he turned and looked at the windshield then when he returned his glance to me he said, "I promise you won't regret it."
We were both happy, but I was still scared. *Would this end like the other relationships or was he the one who would be in our lives forever?*

I had already met his entire family, and Jaylan and I were immediately comfortable with them. Eating Sunday dinner and celebrating birthdays with his family, Jaylan and I had found our new family-away from-family.

Is this real? I've never spent this much time with the family of anyone I've dated. Even with Jason, I didn't get to know his family until after we weren't together. This is so much fun, and it feels so right. His sister, Tammy, and I have so much in common. Jaylan loves Alan, and he's having so much fun with Tammy's boys. Everett's parent's are so much fun, and I love talking to his grandmothers. They are even a lot like my own family.

When Jaylan was in fifth grade, he got another family tree assignment. Easily completing the mom's side of the sheet, Jaylan looked up from the table where he was working and asked, "Ma, do you think it would be okay if I used Everett's family on the other side?" After calling Everett, Jaylan finished the assignment, and I just smiled and stared at his paper. *Will*

Everett be the man we've waited our whole lives for? Please don't let this one end too?

At the end of the school year, Jaylan participated in a 5th grade graduation program. "Ma, you think Everett can come?" he asked a few days before the ceremony.

"I don't know. We'll see," I replied hoping he could attend but not knowing for sure.

The next week Jaylan smiled and waved from his seat on the gymnasium floor of his school when he saw my mother, GG, my brothers, me, and yes, Everett.

I had a graduation too. Although I had completed my coursework for graduate school the previous July and celebrated with a party, my graduation ceremony was not until the following December. Because I attended a satellite campus of the college, my graduation occurred in Jackson, Mississippi at the main campus of Belhaven College. While Everett was still pursuing me, I mentioned the trip that my mother and I would be taking to my graduation in December. He insisted on going. For the first time in my life, I felt real love and support from a man other than my dad. Although he had essentially just met me, I felt like he had known me and my struggles all my life and that he was proud of me and proud to be with me. I was proud to be with him too and thankful to have him in my life.

A couple of years earlier I had sold the little green Sunfire on its last legs. The brakes had been replaced twice, and the air conditioning had gone out forcing me to spend an entire Memphis summer sweating in my car giving me flashbacks of the summer that I volunteered with my mother. At a used car lot, I found my next vehicle and got a deal on a new-to-me gold Lexus RX300 that I never thought I could afford. With my aggressive savings plan always in place, I was able to include a large down payment and even paid the truck off completely in only six months by applying every extra dime I got to the principal payment.

In my new truck, Everett drove my mother, my grandmother, my brother, and of course, my son to Jackson, Mississippi for my MBA graduation ceremony. As I walked across a graduation stage for the third time in my life I looked out into the audience and thanked God for the people who had been there with me from the beginning and for the new blessing he had added to my life.

Lessons Learned:

♥ **Dreams do come true.** Before finding out that I was pregnant, I had dreams. I wanted to go to college. I wanted to be successful. I wanted a career. I wanted to be able to take care of myself and even my parents one day. Never giving up on my dreams, I worked hard and integrated my son into every aspect of my life rather than sacrificing my own life because of him.

♥ **See it to the end.** My eighteen month struggle was worth it when I walked across the stage and received my master's degree. Like in undergraduate school, I considered quitting many times primarily because of childcare challenges. However, I persevered and finished what I started.

♥ **Seek a mentor then become a mentor.** Yes, my son needed a father, but part of what he needed in a father was someone to look up to and someone to show him love and attention outside of me. I found a mentor for him at young age and as he grew, I tried to continuously provide him with role models and mentors. Although in a less formal manner, I found mentors for myself both in college and in my career. As I developed, helping other young women, especially mothers, identify the opportunities before them and showing them the importance of good decisions became a passion for me and the primary purpose of this book.

♥ **Everything happens in due time.** After several unsuccessful relationships, I had given up on finding someone to be there for both my son and me. When I least expected it, I met someone who showed me how to love and to trust again.

A Ring For Me?

The thief's purpose is to steal and kill and destroy. My purpose is to give them a rich and satisfying life. -John 10:10

"I made you some more," Everett grinned as he handed me another box of his fragrant, homemade candles.

"How are you going to make any money if you give them all to me?" I laughed as I accepted his gift.

"I'll make more. Come on Jay," he replied directing Jaylan to hop into his barber chair.

Everett was extremely giving, but I struggled to make him understand my difficult task of balancing my relationship with him with being a mother. Picking Jaylan up from his afterschool program, he was anxious to tell me about his day.

"Ma, we did...and we saw...and I ate...," he poured everything out that he had been holding in all day.

Then my phone rang and I answered, "Hey, Everett."

"Hey, baby. Guess what? I did...I saw...I went...," he started pouring too.

"I just picked Jaylan up, and he's telling me about his day. Let me call you back once we get done with homework, okay?"

"Ah, but I had something to tell you."

Disappointed, he hung up the phone. He was excited about sharing his day with me too.

Returning to Jaylan to finish his story, he looked disappointed too. "Never mind. I forgot what I was saying now," he sighed.

I couldn't win for losing. I wanted to be there for both of them. I wanted to make both of them happy. Why didn't Everett understand that Jaylan had been in school all day and wanted to talk to me, and I never wanted to discourage him from sharing his day with me? Didn't Jaylan just hear me get off the phone so I could talk to him? How am I supposed to balance the two of them?

Although Everett spent a lot of time doing things like taking us to the fair and going to dinner with the two of us, he wanted alone time with me too. Constantly the rope in a game of tug of war, I grappled with how to be both a good mother and a good girlfriend.

However, Everett was a good guy. In fact, he was the best man I had ever had the pleasure of claiming as my own, and I knew we would all be okay. I worked on helping him to be more understanding of my difficult balancing act, and he continued to display all the other characteristics of the man I was so happy that I had decided to give a chance with my heart and my son.

Everett possessed a hard-working attitude and entrepreneurial spirit like no one I had ever met. Observing every move Everett made, my baby was absorbing that spirit too and asked how he could earn money too. He was a busy man always seeking new ventures, but he always made time for me and Jaylan and seemed to enjoy giving us gifts as much as we appreciated receiving them which was why I wasn't surprised when he flooded me with gifts our first Valentine's Day together. Knowing I had never received a gift for Valentine's Day before, he wanted to make sure the day was extra special for me that year. For me, just having him in our lives was enough to make the holiday worthwhile.

My day was filled with surprises starting before I even left my house for work. "Happy Valentine's Day, baby!" he exclaimed kissing me on my cheek and handing me an assortment of body creams.

"Thanks, baby. I love them!" I responded after opening a few of the bottles and smelling the various scents.

"Now this one," he continued grinning and handing me a big striped, pink bag full of cute, little underwear.

"Oooh, thanks, baby! But why are you giving me my gifts now? I'm not giving you yours until tonight."

I was still waiting on the baker at the arena to finish the pan of lemon bars I'd ordered for him. Attending the Grizzlies games with me, he had fallen in love with the lemony dessert that could only be ordered in the luxury suites.

"I'll see you then," he waved me off to work with a mischievous smile.

At work, I received my third gift of a dozen pink and green tulips. In my mind, I could see him smiling and hear him saying, "I bet you didn't know there was such a thing as AKA tulips?" Always a thoughtful gift-giver, he had selected flowers in my sorority colors. The beautiful distraction prevented me from working anymore that day.

At the end of the work day, he called me with a welcomed order, "Go straight home. I'm picking up Jaylan."

With an even heavier than usual lead foot, I rushed home to see why I was instructed to come directly there. Welcomed by two of my favorite men, I entered my kitchen through the garage.

"Just take a seat. Sit back and relax on the couch," Everett continued his instructions.

I didn't say a word and just followed his orders. Trying to open a bottle of Moscato, Everett's blissful mood turned to frustration when he broke the corker. "Ugh, I'll be back. I have to go to the store," he agitatedly stated.

"No, it's okay. We don't have to have wine," I tried to calm him down.

"Yes, we do. I'll be back!" he smiled, at least, then rushed out the door.

When he returned, he finished his preparation. Filling three wine glasses with wine for the two of us and grape juice for Jaylan, he moved on to the salad. Plump, juicy shrimp covered leaves of lettuce on the beautiful salads he created.

"Baby, this looks so good, but I don't like shrimp on my salad," I complained. He looked at me like I had stolen his best friend.

"Okay," he replied and took the plate back.

"Wait," I insisted feeling bad about my response, "let me try it. I've never had it before."

I ate it and actually loved it, but I couldn't understand why he was so frustrated and acting so nervous.

"I have dessert!" I was finally able to get in part of his gift. Handing him the pan of lemon bars, his face lit up, and I knew I had done a good job. The rest of my gifts to him didn't even matter.

Completing the meal, it was time to say goodnight to my first and constant Valentine, Jaylan.

As we sat in my living room, my sweet and thoughtful boyfriend instructed me to relax again as he turned the television on my favorite network, HGTV. He left the room then returned with yet another gift, silky gold sheets that matched my bedroom perfectly! "I'll be right back!" he stated and left the room again and returned with what was surely my final gift, a nice set of bath towels to replace the ones I had used since my college days.

Finally, he took my hand and led me to my bathroom where he had drawn a hot bubble bath for me in my large, Jacuzzi tub. Candles were lit, the music of Floetry played softly and red rose petals were strewn about the room and in the bathtub. Helping me into the tub, he gently washed my back as we talked about the day. He knew I had never had a special Valentine's Day before, and he was ensuring I would never forget that one.

"Okay, I have one more," he eagerly asserted.

"Another gift? Baby, you're doing too much," I responded, but I was anxious to see what the other gift could possibly be.

In the dim candlelight of the room, I could barely see the package he gave me, "Here you go. Open it."

"My hands are wet, baby. Open it for me," I requested.

Kneeling back down by the tub, Everett removed the shrink-wrap on the red velvet, heart-shaped box of chocolates. He knew how much I loved chocolate and had given me thoughtful gifts all day. He struggled with the wrapper for a moment then handed me the box. Pulling the lid off the box, I extended the box towards him to offer him a chocolate before I indulged. He reached in and grabbed what looked to be my largest one!

"How you gonna take my biggest one?!" I exclaimed.

Ignoring me, he got on one knee and grabbed my left my hand fully removing the big chocolate candy I was about to complain about him taking. It was actually a black ring box. My mouth dropped, and my heart started to beat out of my chest.

Looking directly into my eyes he nervously uttered, "Summer, I knew from the moment that I met you that you would be my wife." I laughed a little on the inside because he had actually told me that when he first met me, but I just knew that would never happen because he was not my "type" and made sure he knew it. He continued, "I'm ready to be a father to Jaylan, and I want you to be a mother to Alan. Summer, will you marry me?"

Wiping the sweat from his forehead, he released a relieved smile that said, "Whew, I got it out. I said it. Now there."

In shock, I don't think I even said yes, but then I realized that the lyrics of the song playing at the moment he proposed were "All You Gotta Do is Say Yes". I sat in the tub with my mouth open as I nodded yes until he hugged me and helped me out of the tub.

Everett was excited, and so was I. However, I was more scared than excited. *I love him, but am I ready for this. Lord, what if I marry him and he still leaves. How will Jaylan take this? What am I doing to my child? Well, we're going to be a stepfamily. This is going to be hard. I know this is what I said I wanted, but do I really? Please don't let him change his mind now. I guess we're doing this. Look at him, he's so happy. But I'm so scared. Am I really ready for this?*

Still excited but unsure, we spent the next hour letting everyone know that we were going to get married. I was still in my towel when he ran into Jaylan's room to wake him up and tell him the news. "Young Jay," Everett started, "me and your Mama are about to get married."

Sleepy and shocked, Jaylan didn't know what to think, but he smiled and released a confused, "Okay." The look on his face told me he was happy and the next night when I was talking to my new fiancé on the phone, Jaylan said, "Tell Dad goodnight."

Still sharing the news, we called my mother. She was happy but not really surprised because he had mentioned marriage to her earlier. In fact, he talked about it to me often, but I brushed him off because we had only been dating a few months. My dad didn't even answer the phone that night. It was late, but my new fiancé had already asked for my dad's permission to marry me a month after we started dating when he met him for the first time at Christmas. We also called Everett's family who already knew and had even seen the ring. I called my closest friends, but none of them answered the phone. It was Valentine's night so I figured they were all enjoying the holiday too.

Wearing my ring to work the next day, I was eager to show it off to my friends there. I walked into my co-worker Staci's office where Teresa sat across from her desk. Taking the seat next to them, I made casual conversation asking how the Valentine's Day holiday had gone for them. They shared how they had spent the night before, and then it was my turn to reveal my big news. Lifting my right hand from over my left one, I placed my left hand on Staci's desk expecting screams of excitement. Instead, they both looked at the ring and started laughing. *What? Are they making fun of my ring? Surely not. This ring is beautiful. What's so funny?*

My confused face demanded an explanation. "Summer, congratulations! We're so happy for you, but we already knew!"

"No, you didn't. I called both of y'all last night. No one answered their phones!"

Teresa explained, "Girl, Everett showed us all the ring at Aimee's party. What's so funny is how you came in here acting like you didn't have anything big happen last night." The week before, Everett and I attended a 30th birthday party for my friend Aimee. One by one, Everett had taken my friends outside to show them the ring and share his plans for proposing to me the following week. I couldn't believe my friends were able to keep the secret for a whole week!

"How in the world were you able to keep the secret from me?" I inquired. They responded in unison, "There was no way we were going to ruin that surprise."

Lessons Learned:

♥ **God will fulfill our dreams and bless us abundantly.** Focus on God, doing what is right, and he will bless us with the desires of our hearts.

♥ **There's hope.** I had given up on love and was afraid to even try again. I had also given up on a father figure, or any consistent male figure, in Jaylan's life. God blessed me with both.

Moving On

And we know that God causes everything to work together for the good of those who love God and are called according to his purpose for them. -Romans 8:28

No work was done by me that day. Not only because I was overwhelmed by my engagement, but also because it was my last day working for the team. Part of the reason he had proposed to me the night before was because he wanted me to be able to share it with my co-workers turned family at the Grizzlies before starting my new job.

When I finally finished graduate school, I was ready to test the job market again. Although I loved my job and received a slight raise by earning my MBA, I had been working for the team for almost five years and my salary was only enough to meet my needs and too much of my time was spent at the arena and away from my son. Armed with an MBA degree, I needed to see if I could earn more money at a job that would afford me the opportunity to spend more time with my son. While I did not want to leave the prestige and the perks of working for an NBA team and all the friends I had grown to love, I owed it to Jaylan and to myself to find a job with more regular hours and higher pay.

After a few months of searching, I finally found the second real job of my career. I became the marketing manager for two divisions of a large service franchise company, and I had to tell the Grizzlies goodbye. I set up a meeting with the president of the team, Andy, who I was reporting to at the time since my boss and friend, Marla, had returned to Vancouver. Before leaving, however, Marla gave me a copy of a book about writing called *Bird by Bird* because she knew of my dream to write a book about my journey as a teenage mother.

With Marla gone, I had the difficult task of telling the president that I was leaving. The entire organization consisted of probably less than 200 full-time employees and many of us had been with the team since its move to Memphis. I was one of those people, and I was happy about my career decision but very sad to leave my work family. When I set up the meeting, Andy was not surprised about what I had to tell him. Walking to his office at our appointed meeting time, Andy was on a call and mouthed to me, "I'll come see you in a minute."

A few minutes later, he caught me off guard when he took a seat in an empty chair in my office and sighed, "Okay, lay it on me," as he smiled assuming what I was about to say.

Reluctantly, I told him about the great opportunity I had received and that I would be starting my new job in two weeks.

"Well, Summer, you know I hate to see you leave us. Is there anything I can say to make you stay?"

Knowing that I not only needed more money but also more time, I explained, "I wish I could stay, but I need more time to spend with Jaylan."

Andy adored Jaylan and even hung an autographed photo of Jaylan from his giveaway series photo shoot on the wall in his office next to autographed photos of superstars like Michael Jordan and Magic Johnson. Giving Jaylan books and asking about his grades when he saw him, Andy always encouraged me as a single mother and took a special interest in my child. That meant a lot to me and always made me feel good about working for the team and everything I was doing to support my son.

"I certainly can't argue with that. I'm proud of you, and I'll miss you. They're lucky to have you," he responded making me feel very appreciated for the all the time and effort I had given his organization.

A surprise going away party was held in my honor. All the media partners I had worked with over the years were invited along with the entire Grizzlies staff. A few people made some kind remarks, and then Andy made his speech. Everyone who knows me knows that I am a very emotional person, but I was determined not to cry that day.

Andy proceeded to tell a couple of stories about experiences we had shared working together over the last few years in Memphis. Then, all of sudden, he changed the direction of his speech and began to talk about what he had observed about me as a mother. I had always felt like I was constantly letting my son down and that everything took priority over him. I knew I did my best, but I never felt like I was truly a good mother. However, when Andy relayed his observations, I didn't feel so bad. *Maybe I really am a good mother.* Concluding his speech, Andy chuckled and said, "She's getting hitched and moving on, and I'm extremely proud of her." When Andy stopped talking and reached out to hug me, the group applauded and turned their attention to their wet-faced, red-eyed co-worker, me. I was overwhelmed and never expected Andy to be the one to assure me that I was doing a good job as a mother.

Presenting me with a framed photo of the arena that I broke ground on, gave tours of, and promoted events for, Andy completed the hug he'd started, and I began silently reading some of the notes written by my co-workers on the mat. The party was in the middle of the day and Jaylan was at school and could not attend, but Andy hadn't forgotten about him. "This is for my main man, Jaylan," Andy laughed as he handed me a basketball autographed by the entire Grizzlies basketball team. He continued, "And we'll see you two tonight. Think you got one more game in you?"

As he handed me a pair of floor seats to the game that night, I thought, *Summer, are you sure you want to leave this? Is it too late to change my mind?*

Sitting right next to the Grizzlies bench at the game, Jaylan and I enjoyed the best seats in the house. Jaylan was disappointed that I was leaving the team, but he understood it was best for us. "Ma, why do you have to leave?"

"Baby, I don't have to, but you know how I always get off work late and always have to find somebody to keep you and help you with your homework? I won't have to do that anymore. I'll be able to do more stuff with you now. Plus, I'll even have a little more money and you can start getting an allowance. Doesn't that sound good?"

I got no response, but I knew he would be okay. Looking around the arena, I began to miss my job before I had even left. However, I knew it was time to embrace a new challenge and begin my process of giving more of me to my son.

Lessons Learned:

- ♥ **Education gives you options.** Earning my master's degree provided me with the opportunity to pursue other career options. My degrees and my experience gave me choices for my career and my life, and I didn't have to settle for anything.

- ♥ **Hard work pays off.** From the age of fifteen until I completed graduate school, I was a student, an employee, and a mother. Although I often felt sorry for myself, I didn't let them stop me from moving to change my situation. I didn't sit around feeling sorry for myself

Still Moving Forward

We are confident that as you share in our sufferings, you will also share in the comfort God gives us. -2 Corinthians 1:7

Only two days after leaving the Grizzlies, I started my new job. The company was anxious to get me on board as the position had been vacant for a few months, and the work was not being done.

On my first day, I met my new team, got a tour of the office, and found out where I would be sitting. I was then brought into my new boss's office where we went over a tradeshow schedule for the year. As the new marketing manager, I was expected to attend each of the shows located throughout the country. To my surprise, I would be taking several business trips of up to four days each. *What? You told me there would be no travel on this job? But you don't understand. I can't do that. Do you know how hard it is for me to find someone to keep my son especially through the week when they have to get him to and from school?*

After keeping thoughts to myself for a few minutes, I finally let them out as respectfully as I could.

"Those seem like some really good tradeshows, and I'm sure they'll be great for promoting the brand. I'm just a little confused though. The job description I read said there was no travel involved, and I thought you said the same when I asked you in my second interview. Did I read or hear something wrong?"

Startled by the question that I just had to ask, the director responded sternly saying, "I'm not sure how you might have gotten confused. We'll need you to attend these shows, but you have plenty of time to make arrangements."

Easy for her to say. She didn't have any children and had no idea what life was like for me. Under normal circumstances, I would have jumped at the opportunity to travel for work. However, unlike most of my co-workers who could just pack their bags and leave whenever they wanted and stay gone as long as needed, I always had to make challenging arrangements and find people whose schedule would allow them to take Jaylan to school, pick him up and keep him overnight for several nights. That was never easy. Naomi came through for me as she had done while I was in graduate school, but I thought my job change would eliminate the need to have to rely on others so heavily. Frustrated by my new job on the first day, I struggled to remain optimistic.

I was then taken to the storage room where it was time to get dirty. Yes, I said dirty. Since it was my first day on the job, I had worn a new suit because I was expecting to spend the day meeting people, learning my way around the building, reading papers and just getting acclimated to my new environment. Instead, I began hands-on learning of how to assemble a tradeshow booth. By the time we finished opening boxes, pulling out boards and attaching panels, my new, black suit was dusty brown. While putting together the unwieldy booth, I figured out the reason I was immediately taught how to do it. In addition to standing at the booth for hours during a tradeshow, assembling the booth would be my primary job when I traveled and my first trip was two weeks after my start date.

A bit confused at the disconnect between the job I had accepted and the job I was shown I would have to do, I wondered again if leaving the Grizzlies was the right thing to do. *I have left the job I loved because I needed to work fewer hours and to make more money. What is this job? It's just not what I expected. I don't mind hard work, but I thought I had graduated from some of it. Hauling heavy boxes of pocket schedules to sponsor locations and boxes of T-shirts to radio stations, I was used to manual labor but that was fun. Not only do I have to stress about where Jaylan will be when I travel, but once I get there I have to put this thing together. I messed up. This job just isn't what I expected, and I miss my friends at the Grizzlies too.*

My fiancé and his son, Alan, came over my house that evening. Sending the boys to Jaylan's room, I told Everett about my day and how I felt like I had made a mistake by leaving the Grizzlies.

"Did you pray about the decision before you took the job?" he asked.

"Yeah, but...," I started responding.

"Well, if you got the answer that it was time to leave the Grizzlies and take this job, then you did the right thing. It will all be okay." Looking at the laptop with a cracked screen and the filthy laptop bag with a huge rip on the side that I had been given at work that day, he reminded me of the laptop he had given me for Christmas just a couple of months earlier.

"You already have a laptop so don't worry about that one. Just do your work and come home and get on your better one," he laughed as he rubbed my back reassuring me.

Hearing me say that I would write more if I didn't have to sit at my desk on the computer, he bought me a laptop to encourage me to work on the book I wanted to write about my life as a teenage mother. Handing me a clean laptop bag to carry my work computer, he reminded me of many of the lessons I taught my son especially about making the best of a bad situation. By the end of the night, I was ready to start the next day with a new attitude.

Although the job never compared to my job with the Grizzlies, I appreciated having a new experience and more money to provide for my child but still did not feel like I was where I was supposed to be. Aside from having more travel than I wanted, I just could not seem to get all of my work done during business hours. To finish it, I took my laptop home and worked every night. I figured that once I got over my learning curve, the workload would decrease or I would at least be able to manage it better. However, neither ever happened, and I ended up taking my laptop home every evening for as long as I worked at this company. However after Jaylan said to me, "But Ma, I thought you quit the Grizzlies so you wouldn't have to work so much," I knew I had to make another change.

After a year on the job, I decided to continue my pursuit of finding the right position for me as a single mother. I needed a job that would help me better balance work with my personal life. This time in my job search, I was even willing to take a pay cut to have a job that gave me more time with Jaylan.

At that time, more than ever before, I needed to be with my son. Although he was initially excited about me getting married, he had concerns too. For all of his life, it had just been the two of us. He felt like my fiancé would be taking his place. On top of that, I had begun to let my fiancé help me with disciplining him. As he grew older, Jaylan had gotten to the point where I felt like a man's touch, literally sometimes, was needed. I was thankful to have a man in my life that I knew cared enough about my son to correct him with my direction. However, this correction was often hard for Jaylan to receive, and I questioned if I was doing the right thing by allowing it to happen. *Is it too soon for me to let Everett punish him? Will Jaylan feel betrayed by me? Will he understand why I let him do it? Is Everett really ready for this?*

In the midst of my frustrations with my job, I had to take time out to address my son's fears with the new life we were preparing to have. I had hoped my husband would find me while Jaylan was younger to make acceptance of a new father easier. However, Jaylan was nearly a pre-teen fast-approaching the very age I was when he was born. His voice was changing, and the fuzz on his upper lip became more prominent every day. Accepting Everett's marriage proposal, I realized I was changing my son's life too. In my eyes, it was for the best and he would finally have the father and even the little brother he always wanted.

After walking a couple of silent laps on the walking trail near my house, Jaylan and I rested on a little wooden bench nearly hidden by trees. My worried son inquired, "Ma, why do you have to get married?"

I responded, "Jaylan, I love Everett, and Everett loves you and me. Won't it be so nice to have the family we've both always wanted?"

"But, ma, I think it'll be fine with just me and you." He then laughed a little and sang, "Just the two us, we can make it if we try. Just the two us, you and I."

I smiled slightly and held back the tears that wanted to come. I knew he liked my fiancé, but he was worried that he was losing me. I knew he would never lose me though. Instead, he was gaining a father and a brother.

"Jaylan, now you'll have someone to talk about boy stuff with when you don't feel comfortable talking to me about it, and you'll have a little brother to look up to you and to play games with too. You'll be a great big brother! I promise it is a good thing for us."

"Well, do we have to move? I don't want to leave my friends or change schools. Can he just live there and we live here?" Understandably, he was scared about all the changes coming into his life and starting over with the process of making friends. Honestly, so was I, but I couldn't let my fear show. I knew my fiancé loved us both and was very excited about our families coming together, but this was new for all of us and we had a lot to learn and overcome. Still not convinced that the marriage was a good thing, Jaylan stood up from the bench and then we left the park and headed home. I didn't know what else to say.

I knew it would take time for him to get used to having another man around all the time and to sharing his mother whom he normally had all to himself. It would also take time for him to get used to having a man in his life to love him and to guide him. My soon-to-be husband would have his hands full as well. Stepping in to be a father to a boy who didn't know what it was like to have a father or to have a man around but had always expressed he wanted, and I always knew he needed it, Everett faced a tremendous challenge. We all knew it wouldn't be easy, but none of us had any idea of the magnitude of our decision to become a family.

With dealing with my son's expressed apprehension, my fiance's concealed reservations, planning a wedding, and attending premarital counseling, my job that kept me out of town just got in the way. Knowing how I felt about my job, my fiancé made the suggestion that I apply for a job at FedEx where his mother had worked for several years. That sounded great in theory, but I felt that reality was another story. I had applied for several jobs with FedEx when I completed undergraduate school and again when I was looking to leave the Grizzlies with my

MBA. Since I was never even contacted for an interview in the past, I was discouraged about getting a position with FedEx. However, I had to at least try.

Going to the FedEx website, I applied for a position as a Sr. Marketing Specialist in Small Business Marketing. About two weeks later, I got a phone call from someone in human resources at FedEx requesting to schedule an interview with me. *An interview? I'm already further along than I had ever been with FedEx.* After surviving the panel interview, I didn't expect to hear back from FedEx. I had stumbled over a few of the questions and just did not feel good about my performance. Leaving the interview I thought, *I should have said this or that and should have used this example instead of that one.*

I waited, not so patiently, to hear back from FedEx. Even though I had not done the best I felt I could do during the interview, I tried to remain positive. However, with each day that went by that I did not hear from FedEx, my hopes of getting the job dwindled. Finally, one day while sitting at my desk at work, I got the call that changed my life again.

"Hi, may I speak to Summer Owens?" the voice on the other end of my phone asked.

"This is Summer," I excitedly responded knowing from my caller identification that FedEx was on the other line.

"We'd like to make you an offer. What are your salary requirements?"

Wait a minute. Did you just tell me you want to make me an offer and then asked me what I want to make? Does that mean I can just tell you what I want and you'll still let me have the job?

Responding to her not wanting to overprice myself out of a job but at the same time needing to get the highest amount possible, I gave her a $10,000 range higher than what I was currently earning. She came back with an offer only $1,000 lower than the high end of my range giving me 35% higher salary than at the service company. After accepting the offer and resigning from my other job, I splurged on a spa day to relieve myself of the stress that I was leaving with that job.

Although I could not start my new job until the company's next fiscal year which was two months away, I immediately quit my job at the service company, lived off my savings for two months, and spent the time focusing on Jaylan and planning my wedding. Living below my means and saving aggressively provided me with that opportunity to take a little break.

Lessons Learned:

♥ **Keep climbing.** Keep improving, and continue creating options. Don't get too comfortable because there are always opportunities to improve yourself, your life, and your child's life. Look for them and prepare yourself to receive them.

♥ **Make the best of every situation.** Although I didn't like my new job initially, I learned more about marketing, enhanced my resume and eventually realized that God was setting me up for the next move.

The Successful, Grown Woman

For I know the plans I have for you," says the Lord. "They are plans for good and not for disaster, to give you a future and a hope. -Jeremiah 29:11

Although I didn't weep all day as I had in previous years, my emotions were confused as I thought about the date. It was May 22nd again; my 25th birthday. Hiding in the bathroom part of the day and daydreaming in my office the rest of it, I wiped an occasional tear from my face as I recalled the events of that day ten years earlier. It had been a long ten years full of trials and tribulations, but the decade was also filled with joyous moments of overcoming obstacles. Full of mistakes and regrets, the time was also complete with successes and victories. Ten years prior, a few minutes of a single day changed my life forever. That day was sad and lonely and so were many of the days after it even though I had my child. Finally, I was a grown woman, and I prayed the ten year anniversary of that day would be different.

"Surprise!" Jaylan and Everett exclaimed in unison as I stepped out my back door on to my deck that beautiful, spring evening after an unproductive work day.

Standing over a grill on the deck, Everett stood grinning with a spatula in his hand preparing to flip a salmon filet for me and steaks for him and Jaylan.

"Happy birthday, Baby! Go change clothes so you can sit out here with me Jay," he exclaimed.

Turning towards my son, he gave me his biggest smile and repeated Everett's sentiments, "Happy birthday, Mama! I love you! Are you surprised?"

"Oh yeah, baby. This is the best surprise I've ever gotten!" I stated embracing my son before heading over to plant a big kiss on Everett's cheek.

Early in our relationship, I revealed my secret to Everett letting him know about Jaylan's conception. Determined to give me a new birthday memory, he planned the intimate cookout for me and included Jaylan as well. Although I would never forget what happened to me on my fifteenth birthday, I was thankful for a new event to remember and I looked forward to my future with the man who gave it to me and my baby.

Throughout my celebration, I imagined our new life as husband and wife with our two boys. I was finally about to have the complete family I was rushed into desiring as soon as my son was born.

Shortly after my birthday, Everett bought his own barbershop and his finances increased drastically. Excited about our four-person family, he wanted to buy a new house to give us room to grow. Together we selected a beautiful, five-bedroom, four and a half bathroom home in an exquisite neighborhood near my place of work. We both already owned houses though. Moving into our new home where Jaylan and I would join him after the wedding, he chose to rent his house out, and I chose to sell mine to avoid the hassle of dealing with rental property.

Because I did not want to run the risk of paying my mortgage once I was no longer living in the house, I put my house on the market six months before our wedding date. If selling a house wasn't hard enough, I had the extra challenge of selling it while I was living in it. I woke up early every morning to ensure the house was clean, especially Jaylan's room and bathroom, before I left for work. My house was more popular than I expected and nearly every day someone viewed the property. After only a month on the market, my house was sold.

I earned a decent profit from the sale of my house and put every penny of it in the bank to help fund our debt-free wedding and prepared to move. Selling the house faster than I expected, Jaylan and I had to move out to allow the anxious new owners to take possession of their new home. A good problem to have I figured because I had sold my house, but I had not determined where we would go because I figured I had plenty of time to work that out. My fiancé lived on the other side of town, and my son was still in school so moving in with him was not ideal. Besides, I wanted to do everything right and not live together until after we were married.

Thinking about how I would manage to get Jaylan to school each morning, I called my friend and former co-worker,

Staci, who had initially introduced me to the neighborhood. She understood my predicament and allowed Jaylan and me to move into her house until the end of the school year and my big day with Everett.

I thought, *A temporary move into Staci's house and then I will be in my new home. I can't wait to finally relax and truly be settled.* Although I had lived in my house for nearly five years, I had moved into new dorms and apartments every other year that I had been in Memphis for a total of six moves in less than eight years. Packing and begging for help moving was no fun, and I was anxious to finally be settled in a home where I would live with my new family for many years.

Staci was also my wedding coordinator. As her new roommate, she and I finished planning my wedding while I waited to start my new job.

In the two months before my wedding, I reflected on just how far I had come-from a scared, little fifteen-year old girl to a confident, successful woman. All the while being a mother. I had a great career, a great home, savings and checking accounts, a retirement account, investments and even a college fund for my son. I had learned so much about life and about people, about being a mother, about being a woman, and most importantly, about whom I was and what I wanted in life. My relationship with God had grown, and I was no longer a child with excuses. I was a woman of action who made things happen for myself and my son. Yes, at times I was still afraid, but fear never stopped me from trying and pushing forward towards my dreams.

I thought the only thing I was lacking was a husband for me and father for Jaylan. Marrying Everett would complete the picture. However, next to being a teenage mother, preparing for marriage and the challenges that came with a blended family were the scariest experiences of my life. Although marriage was what I had always wanted, I knew being a wife would not be easy and adjusting to a stepfamily would be a challenge for everyone involved. I also knew that marriage was not the answer to all my problems and that it was not guaranteed to last forever and could even be the biggest let down of all for both my son and me. Ultimately, my life and my eleven-year-old son's life rested on me and my choices. I prayed, many times with my son, that I had made the right decisions and that Everett would not only be with us, but also guide us and protect us as he walked with God and led us into the next phase of our lives. Only God knew what our futures held, but I knew I that the strength and the wisdom I had gained from my life as teenage and single mother had equipped me to deal with whatever was to come.

Lessons Learned:

♥ **Life is simply the sum of our choices.** I made some good ones, but I also made some bad ones. Rather than letting my mistakes determine my future, I used them to make me stronger and wiser and help me shape a better life for me and my son.

♥ **Persevere to the end.** When I became a mother at the age of fifteen to a baby without a father, I thought my life was over. I even thought about ending it. I never imagined that I could have loved my baby so much or realized the dreams I had before getting pregnant.

Conclusion

*All praise to God, the Father of our Lord Jesus Christ. God is
our merciful Father and the source of all comfort.*
-2 Corinthians 1:3-4

Initially devastated by the news and subsequent arrival of
a baby, I changed my attitude from thinking about *what I can't
do* to *what I have to do.* I realized that my success in life was not
only a possibility; it was a necessity. I was a mother, and it was
my job to provide for my son. I had no room for excuses, and no
one wanted to hear them.

My son has been a blessing to me, I cannot imagine my
life without him. He has given true purpose and meaning to my
life and has helped to keep me focused and motivated to be the
best I can be. Going from dependence on family and welfare,
today I am financially independent with multiple accounts
including a college fund for my son and a retirement fund for
myself using the same saving practices implemented early in my
career. Family and friends still play a critical role in our lives and
are needed to help teach and love my son, but I'm thankful that
the decisions I've made have positioned me to take care of
myself and my son on my own.

God took me from a naïve, little girl and turned me into
an intelligent, mature woman with a story to share and,
hopefully, to encourage and inspire other teen mothers. At times
while carrying my son, I did not even want to live. Many teenage
mothers survive the pregnancy but die on the inside giving up
on hopes and dreams or failing to set any goals thinking it is
impossible to achieve them. I am not a spectacular person. I have
not done anything that has not been done before, and that is
exactly why I wanted to share my story. With trust and faith in
God and in oneself, anyone can do what I have done if they
choose.

Every day I seek new challenges for me and for my son,
and right now we are in a new season of our lives. With the
lessons I've learned throughout my life as a teenage and single

mother, I accept the challenges to come and trust God and the ability and strength he gives me to see me through them. Without a doubt, I will experience many of the feelings I've had in my past both good and bad. Life will be hard. I will get overwhelmed. I will try my best and still disappoint my son. I will put other's wants and needs before my own. I will get tired. I will feel like giving up.

However, I will laugh. I will love. I will watch my son grow and mature, and I will continue to mature. I will see both his and my pride in his accomplishments. I will calm his frustrations, and he will sometimes cause and calm mine. I will have more birthday parties for my son, and I will celebrate my own birthday. I will make some people smile, and some people will make me smile.

Some people will make me cry. Some will help me, and some will let me down. I will be up, and I will be down some days, but I will not stop dreaming. I will not stop growing. I will not stop living. I will keep progressing.

One day at a time, I will keep moving forwarding. I will have some failures and some heart breaks, but I will keep trying. I will keep fighting. I will keep succeeding, and I will even look forward to a lifetime of mistakes that will mold me into a better woman and a better mother as I continue to live my remarkable and wonderfully challenging *Life After Birth*.

Other Success Stories

My story is not extraordinary, and it is not unique. However, it is unfortunately more of an exception than the rule for teenage mothers. Life for teenage mothers poses challenges only other teen moms understand, and many of us simply don't know how to overcome those challenges. The expectations of outsiders for teen mothers are typically low, and sadly, many of us have even lower expectations for ourselves. But not all of us give up, and it is my goal to help more of us to pursue fulfilling and rewarding lives.

Following are examples of other teenage mothers who beat the odds and are living successful lives with their children.

Debbie, mother at age 16

When I got pregnant I was sixteen, and I was pretty much the same as I am now-somewhat shy and reserved. When I found out I was pregnant, I was so scared. I did not tell my mother until I was two months into the pregnancy. I do not believe in abortions so that was never an option for me. Resigned to the fact that I was about to be a mother, I decided I had to do the best and be the best mother I could be.

Finishing high school with a child was very hard, but I knew I had to get my diploma. While I was in school, I worked part-time to support my daughter and me. Because her father went to prison when my baby was nine months old, I knew it was all on me to take care of my baby. Today, my daughter is 11 years old, and her father is still in prison so he has never played a role in her life. I did have a few people that would help but I just made up my mind to work and do whatever it took to support us.

Being a teenage mother, I missed out on everything after I had her and my life changed so much. I realized life was no longer just about me. It is all about your child and doing what is best for them. No more going out to parties or spending money on meaningless things. I had to learn how to budget. I had to learn how to be a good mother. I also had to watch who I dated who I brought in and out of her life. I did not want her getting attached to or even seeing alot of men. I usually ended up in long relationships, but the guys never met her unless I felt they were important and would be around long enough.

After I became a mother, I found that I didn't fit in with most of my friends anymore. I realized that being a mother changed me for the better. I became a lot more mature because when I became a mother, I became an adult and had to grow up. I will always miss my years not being able to be that carefree teenager, but it turned me into a better person overall. I see a lot of mistakes and bad decisions that my friends made, and I did not make those decisions because I knew I had to be there for my daughter. I had someone to care for; someone who needed me at home.

I got married when my daughter started kindergarten, and it has affected us a lot. Life was easier because I had the help I needed with my daughter; however, when you have been on your own so long taking care of your child, it is hard to let go and allow someone to help you. I had to learn how to not only be a mother, but also a wife. Being a mother, I had control over what my daughter did and no one else, and it was hard letting that go. Once I got past that issue, everything fell into place and I appreciated my husband and my marriage even more. I had someone to help with homework and other needs and someone to be that father and husband we both needed.

Today, my daughter is in the sixth grade, and we added another child to the family in 2008. We are just living day to day, but we are so thankful. We are so blessed. I have a good job working 40 hours a week in customer service, and the rest of my time is devoted to my family.

Who would have thought this sixteen year old struggling to take care of herself and her baby would end up happily married with a great husband? My advice is to listen to your instincts and to be yourself. I always wanted to be liked and would step outside my chracter to do so. I just wanted to fit in. Cherish your body and respect yourself. Remember if your boyfriend loves you he should love you enough to wait until you are ready for sex and be prepared to deal with the consequences. I look back at my life and realize that if only I would have made my own choices, life would have been a lot easier for me. I cannot say that having my baby was a mistake because she changed me for the better. Although sometimes it was a struggle, when I look at her and my family now I know that maybe that was just what I needed. I had faith and determination that everything would work out for me and that my life was planned and somehow, some way we would be okay.

Tasha, mother at age 17

Before I got pregnant I considered myself a good girl. I never got into trouble and always did what I was told to do. This certainly was not supposed to happen to me. I had a plan for my life, and it did not include being a mother so soon. I was not a wild girl and did not have sex a lot, but this time I got pregnant.

I was seventeen years old, a senior in high school, and literally had my entire life ahead of me. Three months pregnant when I found out, I struggled with telling my parents. Somehow in my mind I thought that if I did not deal with it, it would go away. Crazy I know, but that was how I felt. On top of that, I was not with my daughter's father. In fact, I had not even spoken to him in about three months. I knew he would either not believe I was pregnant or say he was not the father because we had not been in contact for so long. All alone, I felt this pregnancy was the worst thing that could have ever happened to me. I felt like dying would be easier than having to deal with this.

Fortunately, when I found out I was pregnant, it was the end of the school year and I graduated. I was not sure what I wanted to do about college though. Finally, I decided to attend a two year college so that I could get a decent job to support my baby. It definitely was not easy working, going to school and being a mother, but I did what I had to do.

Having a baby so young, my life that was just about to truly begin had somewhat ended, at least this is how I felt. All of my friends were away at college being young adults having fun and only worrying about themselves. I, on the other hand, was then an eighteen year old mother and to me there was nothing fun about that. It was hard for me to date because I had a small child and could not leave her home with my mother. If I went anywhere I had to take her with me and was really limited on what and where I could go. Life was hard because I did not have a lot of money, and her dad did not help me at all. It feels really bad when your baby needs diapers and you don't have the money you need to take care of her every day needs. I had to depend on my parents a lot financially, but this was not fair to them. They had not planned on having another child or had the finances for it, so it not only made life hard for me, but it made life hard for my family as well.

I could not hinder my family too long. I had to grow up. I think I had to mature to a lot of situations most girls my age knew nothing about. I can say it has made me a good mother and more responsible when it comes to my daughter. Being a mother has opened my eyes more, and it helps me to talk to my daughter about teenage pregnancy. I share my story with her to let her know it is not as easy as people may think.

When I got married, it helped tremendously. I always felt so alone and that I was going through life by myself. I had my parents, but it was not the same as having a man in my life or someone to take care of me for a while. My daughter finally had a father and she did not have to hear about her friends' fathers and feel left out anymore.

Now my daughter is eleven years old and attending middle school. She is a smart girl, and I am so proud to be her mother. I recently had another child and actually got to enjoy the process of doing it right with a husband, my own home, and a good job. This time around, I was happy to be pregnant and got to prepare for my baby with his dad. There will always be a piece of me that wishes both my children had the same father because I know my daughter sometimes feels left out because her biological father has not been there for her and she wishes he would. Although even this adjustment has not been seamless,

I am thankful for my husband and the role he has played as her father.

Although my life has been a struggle, I use what I've learned to teach my daughter. As young girls and as women, our lives are so precious. Now don't get me wrong, I love my daughter with all the breath in my body. However, I definitely wish I could have done a lot of things differently. I am thirty years old and never went to college for what I really wanted to do. Now later in life, I am trying to fix all the things I messed up as a young woman all because I had to be a mother way before I was ready. I encourage all young girls to listen to your parents, enjoy school, enjoy your friends, and enjoy being a child. You have plenty of time to be an adult and it is not an easy road once you get on and you can't get off. Please value your education and always put God first and whatever situation you get into, he can help you get out. When you do have children, you want it to be the right way. You want to be able to enjoy that time because it is too special to go through alone and you want it to be on God's time. However, if you already have a baby, learn from your mistakes and teach your child. Push forward and make the best of your situation by not giving up.

Tammy M., mother at age 14

I am a firm believer that the choices we make and how we handle the events of our lives shape us into the individuals we become. I feel very fortunate to have been a part of a loving, caring, giving family. The opportunities I have been given far exceed the challenges. But one of the biggest challenges I have been faced with was my pregnancy at age fourteen. I must also state it was one of the biggest blessings of my life that shaped me into the woman I am today.

The minute I accepted I was "really" pregnant, I immediately began to analyze the situation and devise my plan of action. This analytical characteristic is still an inherent trait I use and abuse constantly in my life! Meaning, I can over analyze the simplest of tasks if I have a lot of uncertainty of the end result. The one decision I couldn't make was how to tell my parents. As the baby of the family, I had always been very well behaved, loving, reserved and an all around good child, this was going to turn my parent's world upside down and completely devastate our family. I couldn't do it. So, my answer was to leave a note and leave town with the baby's father. Probably not the best decision because what would we do as parents, at age fourteen and fifteen in a different town, a different state?

After several days, we did come home and boy was that a moment that I will never forget! The look of despair and relief all in one expression on my mother's face and the look I never received from my father because of the shame. As daddy's girl, this feeling of shame and complete, utter disappointment has never completely left me and it was probably THE defining moment in my life. Because, it was at that moment this challenge God had presented me with would become the driving force of my determination and strength of character to succeed.

Summar Lyn was born January 5th, 1985 on a cold, snowy winter day at Jackson Madison County Hospital in Jackson, TN. She was 8lbs 2oz, healthy, beautiful and it brought a bit of life back to our family once again. Within a week of her birth, I was back in school to make sure I didn't get too far behind. Pregnancy was not going to stop me from getting an education and my education was not going to be sub-par or minimal just a lot harder to attain with a baby in tow. I attended high school until I had Summar, continued with my honors classes post-baby as planned and committed to finishing school with the best academic scores possible. I graduated in 1987, on time, ranked 26 in my class!

I have countless stories of the struggles, obstacles, and adversity that I would encounter. Each situation would mold me and empower me to be the best I can be and remain determined to succeed. I was ridiculed, ignored, looked down upon and chastised because of the stigma that ensued from being a teenage mother. Was it hard? Yes! Was it frustrating? Yes! Was it sad? Yes! Did I fail? Absolutely not!

In the last twenty-four years, I have accomplished so much in my life but the driving force that began and kept me motivated, encouraged and determined was that sweet little baby girl, Summar Lyn. I knew from the moment I saw that face that it was MY responsibility to care for her, raise her, provide for her and be an exemplary example of success, exposing her to a discernible example of independence, self-sufficiency and responsibility so important for a life of accomplishment and affirmative individual growth. This driving force only magnified when I added Logan, my son in 1988 and my most recent precious gem, Zoe Grace in 2000.

I have continued down a path of learning and development, receiving my bachelor's degree with a double major in 1991. I have successfully advanced in my career over the past 18 years with wonderful opportunities across several companies. Currently, I am a Marketing Manager with one of the world's best and most noted brands, FedEx. My most recent accomplishment has been the completion of my MBA from the University of Mississippi. Of all these accomplishments, the biggest success and reward has been the gift God has given me through the title of "Motherma".

Each step of the way has included a fair share of challenges that at times were frustrating and seemed insurmountable. But, you learn the reward is worth it and as I continually tell my children, you can do ANYTHING you want in life. It may not be easy but with sound determination and commitment, all things are possible.

In closing, I can't write one word of this without thanking my parents for their unending love, support and encouragement; my sister for always being there to help me for the small and BIG needs required of a young, single mother; my loving husband, Shawn, of nine years – WOW, how good it feels to have unwavering love and finally to the three beautiful seeds of life that bring me unending joy, Summar, Logan and Zoe.

Persevere, live life knowing God has a plan and as all things happen for a reason. I have lived my life by one key bible verse: *I can do ALL things through Christ who strengthens me. Philippians 4:13*

May God bless you and keep you through all phases of your life delivering both challenges and rewards to mold you into the best person possible.

Ardewa, mother at age 14

When I was in high school, I was quiet, but outgoing as well, like I am now. I was a choir member and also ran track my freshman year of high school. When I was in the ninth grade, I got pregnant at the age of 14. I was a virgin, and I let people influence me. I was scared, worried and disappointed in a sense because I felt my life was over. I did not know how I was going to raise a child when I couldn't even take care of myself, especially financially.

I did not tell my mother I was pregnant until I was into my second month of pregnancy. She had already noticed the difference in me anyway. I had begun to gain weight and slept a lot. I was fortunate that my baby's father was there for me during and after my pregnancy. He helped me. Some girls aren't so lucky to have that, but I was. Even his mother and my mother helped even though they were disappointed and upset with us.

I had a premature baby born in my seventh month of pregnancy. When I went into labor, I stayed in the hospital for a month because they were trying to keep me from delivering too early. My baby's lungs were not fully developed yet. They were able to keep me from delivering for a few weeks, but then finally I had him. He was 3lbs and 4oz. I actually almost died having my baby because he was coming out breeched, feet first. I thank God we came out just fine though.

After my baby came home and after I healed, I went back to school. My mother supported me and promised me that she would not let me be a drop out. She also got me a job working with her part time as a Nurses Assistant. I went to school and worked weekend shifts at night. In May of 1997, I graduated from high school.

My son is now fifteen years old and in the tenth grade. I told him what I went through and that I did not want to see him be a father early because it is hard and you will miss out on a lot of things in your teenage life.

I am now a successful business owner and married with three other children. Without God and love from family and friends, I could not have stayed focused. I would not have made it, but I did because I did not give up. My advice to all the young people is to wait until you are married to have sex and to practice abstinence because life is hard as a teenage mother. However, if you have already become a mother, trust God and work hard and you can make it.

Tammy H., mother at age 15

Before I got pregnant, I was the type of girl that wanted to fit in. However, I was a little on the shy side. I used to sneak and talk to boys on the phone because my parents wouldn't allow me to. Most of my peers were already having sex. I was fourteen when I got pregnant, and I was very afraid to tell my mother that I missed my cycle so I told my stepmother and she took me to the doctor. She recommended an abortion, but my mother didn't agree. My mother said that I would have to do the responsible thing and raise my own baby.

While I was pregnant, I attended a school for pregnant girls. I had my son two days after I turned fifteen and then returned to the school for teenage pregnant girls because they also offered child care while we were in class. I attended throughout my freshman year and returned to a normal high school my sophomore year. While I was in high school, I worked in the evening because I needed money to support my son. My mother kept him while I worked most evenings after school and some weekends. Working a part-time job, I did what I could to be responsible for my own actions, and my mother helped me a lot. I always had my son unless I was at work or school. It was not by force, but I felt that I had to be responsible.

Once I graduated from high school, I moved out on my own and went straight into the workforce without attending college. I worked a couple of jobs and realized I needed more education to get ahead. Five years after completing high school, I attended a two year technical school and obtained an Associate Degree in Business Administration.

It was all on me. My son's father was never there for me. He refused to own up to his responsibility. He continued to sleep around with other girls and also told people that my son was not his baby. The only reason he paid $40 a month in child support was because his mother made him get a job at McDonald's. She then took him to Juvenile Court to have him place himself on child support, but we all know that $40 was not much help.

My whole life changed. I made the volleyball team in high school, but I never got to play. My step mother made me get a job to support my child. I was so hurt, but she was right. I couldn't hang out like others my age did either. People that knew I had a baby didn't want their daughters or even their sons socializing with me. I was frustrated and sometimes felt like an outsider. However, I realized that having a child at such a young age can either make or break you. I decided I would not let it break me. In fact, it made me a much more responsible and mature person. I had to grow-up quick.

When my son was eight years old, I married my high school sweetheart. We had been dating since my son was about one year old. I was blessed because when we married they already had a good relationship. From day one, my husband took my son under his wings and treated him just like he was his son. I thank God for looking over me and giving me that peace.

Today I am working in the accounting field in the hospitality industry. I enjoy what I do and the time it allows me to spend with my family. My son is a senior in high school, and my husband and I have since had two more boys. I talk to them all the time about not making the same mistakes that I made. I encourage them to not have sex, and I tell them about the consequences that could come from having sex. Because I remember my weaknesses at his age, I also tell them that his friends don't have to know what they are doing and to not feel pressure to have sex. My friends and my desire to fit in caused me to miss out on so many opportunities.

However, I did not allow my mistakes in high school determine the outcome for the rest of my life. Through hard work, perseverance and prayer, I am now living a happy, fulfilling life with my wonderful family.

SirKeather, mother at age 14

In the ninth grade at the age of fourteen, I became pregnant with my son. I wasn't a "fast" girl. Instead, I was very reserved and quiet. I came from a single-parent household. I watched my mother escape an abusive marriage to struggle to provide for me and my four siblings. I was the oldest girl and that came with alot of responsibility. So when I became pregnant, I was petrified to tell my family. Not necessarily because of the shame, because I was a product of a teen mom, but basically because it was already hard and I had added to the hardship by bringing another mouth into the house to feed. I actually told my mother's best friend who then told my mom that I was pregnant. I was staying with my aunt at the time and would come home on the weekends to be with my siblings, so my mom had called me and told me that when I came home that weekend we needed to talk. I cried the whole week and when I did come home, I had decided that I didn't want to be a burden to my family with this baby and that I wanted to have an abortion.

I was very adamant about my position and my mom went along with me. We talked to my son's father who said that he didn't touch me and I wasn't pregnant by him. Needless to say, there was no support there so we left him saying that it didn't matter if he was the father or not because I wasn't keeping the baby anyway. My mom made my appointment for the abortion. I went to have the procedure done and didn't go through with it. Something came over me and I just couldn't do it. My mom never wanted me to have the abortion, but since it was my decision and my life, she stood behind me. When I decided not to get it done, she stood beside me. When I pushed my son out, on April 4, 1991, she was right with me.

I had my son a month early. Although he was premature, he was okay. My son's father never knew that I didn't terminate the pregnancy so once he found out I was still pregnant he had his brother to ask me, was it his baby. I told him to tell him, that since he didn't touch me like he said to me and my mom, it was my baby. With time, I finally did talk to him and when our son was born, he brought over a big bag of things for him.

Having a child as a child was truly hard. But I guess, I had some earthly angels to help. I completed ninth grade by way of home bound teaching, so I never fell behind in my studies. My nurse practitioner was the wife of a local lawyer, who gave me a job after school at his law firm. At the time I thought I wanted to be a lawyer. I also was a participant of a government summer program called JTPA and worked at the local health department and after the summer ended, they were so impressed with my work they hired me. Even though I was a teen mom , I worked two jobs and went to school to provide for him. I had the type of parents (mom & grand mom) who gave baby sitting services for work and school only. I had a social life, but my son was right beside me. Football, basketball games, mall trips, he was right by my side or in his stroller.

The road has not been easy, I was very focused and determined to succeed and not be a statistic as so many of my fellow classmates who started out with me would become. Even though I knew the odds were against me, being a black, single, teen mom, I always strived to be the very best that I could be. I did finish high school on time and went to a local business college and hair school. I had the option to go off to college, but I didn't want to leave my son. I stayed home, worked and focused on raising him. His dad was in and out of his life, and we even eventually got married, but later divorced.

Today, my son is an eighteen year old college freshman. He is a very fine, respectable, upstanding young man. I am so proud to call him my son. He has never given me a bit of trouble. I have never been in a courtroom with him, and he is not a teen parent. I did have the blessing of motherhood again, but God loved them more and called my sweet daughters back home - Kennedi Aurelia in 2005 and Acacia Malae in 2007. I am in my last ten hours of college and look forward to obtaining my Bachelor's of Business Administration degree in Business soon. I also plan to obtain my master's degree before my son finishes his bachelor's degree.

Some people look at me and say I'm a success story. I say, it's my journey, my struggles. I understood early in my life that my background may influence who I am , but I am responsible for whom I become. Some of us have it easy, some of us have it hard. I just know that my son, made me into the woman, I am. My determination, my focus, my smile- I did it all for him. He is my motivator and I am his teacher. You lead by example and the choices that I have made in my life are really the only ones that define me.